Title: "Mastering Natural Language Processing: A Comprehensive Guide from Basics to

Deployment"

TABLE
Of
contents:

Introduction:

Embark on an enlightening journey through the realms of Natural Language Processing (NLP) with this comprehensive guide. From understanding the basics to deploying advanced models, each step is demystified. The book integrates theoretical concepts with hands-on coding, utilizing Google Colab for a seamless learning experience.

Chapter 1: NLP Fundamentals

Uncover the essence of NLP, exploring tokenization, stemming, and lemmatization. Dive into the world of word embeddings and sentiment analysis, laying the foundation for the practical journey ahead.

Chapter 2: Text Preprocessing

Learn the art of preparing textual data with comprehensive preprocessing techniques. From handling missing values to encoding categorical variables, this chapter ensures your data is ready for the modeling stage.

Chapter 3: Exploratory Data Analysis (EDA)

Delve into the nuances of EDA for NLP. Visualize word frequencies, n-grams, and sentiment distributions. Gain insights into your data to inform effective modeling decisions.

Chapter 4: Model Building

Navigate through a variety of NLP models, from traditional machine learning approaches to cutting-edge deep learning architectures. Code explanations ensure clarity, even for readers new to the technical landscape.

Chapter 5: Model Evaluation

Understand the metrics that gauge model performance. ROC curves, accuracy scores, and precision-recall curves are demystified, empowering readers to assess their models effectively.

Chapter 6: Model Deployment

Take your NLP models from the notebook to real-world applications. Understand deployment strategies and witness the seamless integration of your model into practical scenarios.

Chapter 7: Comparative Analysis

Consolidate your learning by comparing different NLP models. Evaluate the ROC, accuracy, and other metrics to determine the best-suited model for a given task.

Chapter 8: Holistic NLP Mastery

Summarize your NLP journey, reflecting on the fundamental concepts mastered. Even non-technical readers find this chapter engaging, as NLP becomes as accessible as a piece of cake.

Conclusion:

Congratulations! NLP has been unveiled, and you are now equipped to conquer the world of Natural Language Processing. This holistic guide ensures both technical and non-technical readers find value in understanding, applying, and mastering NLP concepts. Happy coding!

CHAPTER 1:

NLP Fundamentals

Welcome to the intriguing world of Natural Language Processing (NLP), where the essence of language meets the power of technology. In this chapter, we will unravel the fundamental concepts that form the backbone of NLP. From tokenization and stemming to lemmatization, we'll delve into the building blocks of processing human language. As we progress, we'll take a deep dive into the captivating realms of word embeddings and sentiment analysis, laying a robust foundation for the practical journey that lies ahead.

Unveiling the Essence of NLP

Natural Language Processing, often abbreviated as NLP, is a field at the intersection of computer science, artificial intelligence, and linguistics. It empowers machines to understand, interpret, and generate human-like text, enabling seamless communication between humans and computers.

Tokenization: Breaking Language into Pieces

The journey begins with tokenization, the process of breaking down a text into smaller units, known as tokens. These tokens can be as granular as individual words or as broad as entire sentences. Tokenization is a crucial step, providing a structured foundation for subsequent NLP tasks.

Python code

```
# Python Code for Tokenization
import nltk
nltk.download('punkt')
from nltk.tokenize import word_tokenize

text = "Uncover the essence of NLP, exploring tokenization, stemming, and lemmatization."
tokens = word_tokenize(text)
print("Tokens:", tokens)
```

In this code snippet, we utilize the Natural Language Toolkit (nltk) to tokenize a given text, breaking it into individual words or punctuation marks. The resulting tokens form the basis for further linguistic analysis.

Stemming and Lemmatization: Simplifying Words

Stemming and lemmatization are techniques employed to reduce words to their base or root form. Stemming involves removing prefixes or suffixes, while lemmatization aims for a more meaningful transformation by considering the word's context.

Python code

```
# Python Code for Stemming and Lemmatization
from nltk.stem import PorterStemmer, WordNetLemmatizer
```

```python
# Stemming
stemmer = PorterStemmer()
stemmed_words = [stemmer.stem(word) for word in tokens]
print("Stemmed Words:", stemmed_words)


# Lemmatization
lemmatizer = WordNetLemmatizer()
lemmatized_words = [lemmatizer.lemmatize(word) for word in tokens]
print("Lemmatized Words:", lemmatized_words)
```

Here, the PorterStemmer and WordNetLemmatizer from nltk showcase the application of stemming and lemmatization, respectively. These processes aid in simplifying words to their essential forms, facilitating efficient language analysis.

Word Embeddings: Mapping Words to Vectors

As we navigate deeper into NLP, the concept of word embeddings takes center stage. Word embeddings are numerical representations of words in a continuous vector space. They capture semantic relationships, allowing algorithms to understand context and similarities between words.

Python code

```python
# Python Code for Word Embeddings with Word2Vec
from gensim.models import Word2Vec


# Dummy Corpus for Training Word2Vec
corpus = [
    "uncover essence NLP exploring tokenization stemming lemmatization",
```

```
    "dive world word embeddings sentiment analysis",
    "lay foundation practical journey ahead"
]
```

```
# Tokenizing Sentences in the Corpus
tokenized_sentences = [word_tokenize(sentence) for sentence in corpus]
```

```
# Training Word2Vec Model
word2vec_model = Word2Vec(sentences=tokenized_sentences, vector_size=50, window=3, min_count=1, workers=4)
```

```
# Access Word Embeddings
word_embeddings = word2vec_model.wv
print("Word Embedding for 'NLP':", word_embeddings['NLP'])
```

In this code snippet, we employ the Word2Vec model from the gensim library to train word embeddings on a dummy corpus. The resulting word vectors encapsulate semantic relationships and can be accessed for individual words.

Sentiment Analysis: Decoding Emotions in Text

Sentiment analysis is a captivating aspect of NLP that involves determining the sentiment or emotion expressed in a piece of text. This can range from positive and neutral to negative sentiments.

Python code

```
# Python Code for Sentiment Analysis with TextBlob
from textblob import TextBlob
```

```
# Dummy Text for Sentiment Analysis
```

```
text_for_sentiment = "This book on NLP fundamentals is incredibly
insightful and engaging!"

# Analyzing Sentiment
blob = TextBlob(text_for_sentiment)
sentiment_polarity = blob.sentiment.polarity
sentiment_subjectivity = blob.sentiment.subjectivity

print("Sentiment Polarity:", sentiment_polarity)
print("Sentiment Subjectivity:", sentiment_subjectivity)
```

In this example, we leverage TextBlob, a powerful library for NLP, to analyze the sentiment of a given text. The sentiment polarity indicates the sentiment's positivity or negativity, while subjectivity measures the degree of personal opinion.

Conclusion

This chapter has been a captivating exploration of NLP fundamentals, from breaking down language into tokens to understanding the emotional tone through sentiment analysis. We've touched on the essence of NLP, paving the way for a practical journey filled with hands-on coding and insightful explanations.

As we proceed through the subsequent chapters, the foundational knowledge gained here will serve as a compass, guiding us through more advanced NLP concepts and applications. Stay engaged, keep coding, and let the journey into the fascinating world of Natural Language Processing continue!

CHAPTER 2:

Text Preprocessing

Welcome to the intricate art of preparing textual data, a crucial phase in the Natural Language Processing (NLP) journey. In this chapter, we embark on a comprehensive exploration of preprocessing techniques. Our goal is to transform raw text into a clean, structured format, ensuring that the data is primed and optimized for subsequent modeling stages.

Understanding Text Preprocessing

Text preprocessing is akin to preparing a canvas for a masterpiece. It involves a series of steps to clean, refine, and standardize textual data, making it suitable for analysis and modeling. From handling missing values to encoding categorical variables, each preprocessing step contributes to the creation of a robust dataset.

Handling Missing Values

Missing values are like blank spots on the canvas, and addressing them is essential for a complete picture. In NLP, missing values can disrupt the coherence of the text. Let's explore methods to handle these gaps in the textual landscape.

Code Example: Handling Missing Values

Python code

```python
# Python Code for Handling Missing Values in Text Data
import pandas as pd

# Dummy DataFrame with Textual Data
data = {'Text': ['The quick brown fox', 'jumps over the lazy dog', None,
'In the jungle, the mighty jungle']}
df = pd.DataFrame(data)

# Display Original DataFrame
print("Original DataFrame:")
print(df)

# Handling Missing Values (Filling with Empty String)
df['Text'].fillna('', inplace=True)

# Display DataFrame after Handling Missing Values
print("\nDataFrame after Handling Missing Values:")
print(df)
```

In this code snippet, we use a dummy DataFrame to simulate textual data. The missing value is filled with an empty string, ensuring data continuity.

Tokenization Revisited

Tokenization, introduced in the previous chapter, remains a cornerstone of text preprocessing. It involves breaking down text into smaller units, usually words or subwords. Revisiting tokenization during preprocessing helps maintain consistency in the treatment of textual data.

Code Example: Tokenization during Preprocessing

Python code

```python
# Python Code for Tokenization during Text Preprocessing
from nltk.tokenize import word_tokenize
from sklearn.feature_extraction.text import CountVectorizer

# Dummy Corpus for Tokenization
corpus = [
    "The quick brown fox",
    "jumps over the lazy dog",
    "In the jungle, the mighty jungle"
]

# Tokenization with NLTK
tokenized_sentences = [word_tokenize(sentence) for sentence in corpus]
print("Tokenized Sentences with NLTK:")
print(tokenized_sentences)

# Tokenization with Scikit-Learn's CountVectorizer
vectorizer = CountVectorizer()
tokenized_count_vectorizer = vectorizer.fit_transform(corpus)
print("\nTokenized Sentences with CountVectorizer:")
print(tokenized_count_vectorizer.toarray())
```

This code illustrates two approaches to tokenization. The first utilizes

NLTK for sentence tokenization, breaking down each sentence into individual words. The second uses Scikit-Learn's CountVectorizer to create a tokenized representation of the textual data.

Removing Stopwords and Punctuation

Stopwords and punctuation are akin to noise in the artistic process. Removing them during text preprocessing enhances the focus on meaningful words. Stopwords are commonly used words (e.g., "the," "is," "and") that do not contribute significant meaning, while punctuation adds clutter.

Code Example: Removing Stopwords and Punctuation

Python code

 # Python Code for Removing Stopwords and Punctuation in Text Data

from nltk.corpus import stopwords

import string

 # Dummy Sentence

sentence = "The quick brown fox jumps over the lazy dog."

 # Tokenization

tokens = word_tokenize(sentence)

 # Removing Stopwords

stop_words = set(stopwords.words('english'))

filtered_tokens = [word for word in tokens if word.lower() not in stop_words]

 # Removing Punctuation

filtered_tokens = [word for word in filtered_tokens if word not in string.punctuation]

```
print("Original Tokens:")
print(tokens)
print("\nFiltered Tokens (Without Stopwords and Punctuation):")
print(filtered_tokens)
```

In this snippet, we utilize NLTK's stopwords and Python's string library to remove stopwords and punctuation, streamlining the textual data.

Encoding Categorical Variables: Label Encoding and One-Hot Encoding

Textual data often includes categorical variables that require numerical representation for modeling. Two common techniques are label encoding and one-hot encoding.

Code Example: Encoding Categorical Variables

Python code

```
# Python Code for Label Encoding and One-Hot Encoding in Text Data
from sklearn.preprocessing import LabelEncoder, OneHotEncoder

# Dummy DataFrame with Categorical Textual Data
data = {'Category': ['Fiction', 'Non-Fiction', 'Sci-Fi', 'Non-Fiction', 'Sci-Fi']}
df_category = pd.DataFrame(data)

# Display Original DataFrame
print("Original DataFrame:")
print(df_category)

# Label Encoding
```

```
label_encoder = LabelEncoder()
df_category['Category_LabelEncoded'] = label_encoder.fit_transform(df_category['Category'])

# Display DataFrame after Label Encoding
print("\nDataFrame after Label Encoding:")
print(df_category)

# One-Hot Encoding
one_hot_encoder = OneHotEncoder(sparse=False, drop='first')
one_hot_encoded = one_hot_encoder.fit_transform(df_category[['Category']])
df_category_one_hot = pd.concat([df_category, pd.DataFrame(one_hot_encoded, columns=['Fiction', 'Sci-Fi'])], axis=1)

# Display DataFrame after One-Hot Encoding
print("\nDataFrame after One-Hot Encoding:")
print(df_category_one_hot)
```

In this example, we use a dummy DataFrame with categorical textual data. Label encoding assigns numerical labels to each category, while one-hot encoding creates binary columns for each category.

Lemmatization during Preprocessing

Lemmatization, introduced in the previous chapter, finds its place in text preprocessing. It ensures that words are transformed into their base or root form, contributing to uniformity in the textual landscape.

Code Example: Lemmatization during Text Preprocessing
Python code

```python
# Python Code for Lemmatization during Text Preprocessing
from nltk.stem import WordNetLemmatizer

# Dummy Sentence
sentence = "Dogs are running in the park, chasing the balls."

# Tokenization
tokens = word_tokenize(sentence)

# Lemmatization
lemmatizer = WordNetLemmatizer()
lemmatized_tokens = [lemmatizer.lemmatize(word) for word in tokens]

print("Original Tokens:")
print(tokens)
print("\nLemmatized Tokens:")
print(lemmatized_tokens)
```

This snippet showcases the application of lemmatization to transform words in a sentence into their base forms, promoting consistency.

Conclusion

This chapter has been an immersive journey into the intricate art of text preprocessing. From handling missing values to encoding categorical variables, each step plays a vital role in preparing textual data for the modeling stage. As we conclude this chapter, armed with a refined dataset, we set the stage for the next phase of our NLP adventure—model building.

In the upcoming chapters, we will leverage the preprocessed textual data to build, evaluate, and deploy powerful NLP models. Stay *engaged, practice the code in Google Colab for a hands-on experience, and let the art of text preprocessing become second nature in your NLP endeavors. Happy coding!*

CHAPTER 3:
Exploratory Data Analysis (EDA)

Welcome to the illuminating world of Exploratory Data Analysis (EDA) for Natural Language Processing (NLP). In this chapter, we embark on a journey of discovery, diving deep into the nuances of EDA specific to textual data. Our mission is to unravel the patterns, structures, and sentiments within the textual landscape. By visualizing word frequencies, exploring n-grams, and understanding sentiment distributions, we equip ourselves with invaluable insights to guide effective modeling decisions.

Unveiling the Power of EDA in NLP

Exploratory Data Analysis is the compass that guides our understanding of the data. In the context of NLP, EDA unveils the richness of textual information, helping us make informed decisions during the modeling phase.

Visualizing Word Frequencies

Words are the building blocks of language, and their frequencies hold valuable information about the dataset. Visualizing word frequencies allows us to identify common terms, potential stopwords, and the overall textual landscape.

Code Example: Visualizing Word Frequencies

Python code

 # Python Code for Visualizing Word Frequencies in Text Data

from wordcloud import WordCloud

import matplotlib.pyplot as plt

 # Dummy Textual Data

text_data = "Explore the nuances of Exploratory Data Analysis for Natural Language Processing. Dive deep into the world of NLP and gain insights."

 # Generate Word Cloud

wordcloud = WordCloud(width=800, height=400, background_color='white').generate(text_data)

 # Display Word Cloud

plt.figure(figsize=(10, 5))

plt.imshow(wordcloud, interpolation='bilinear')

plt.axis('off')

plt.show()

This code snippet utilizes the WordCloud library to generate a visual representation of word frequencies in a given text. The resulting word cloud provides an immediate glimpse into the prominent terms within the data.

Exploring N-grams: Uncovering Syntactic Structures

N-grams are contiguous sequences of n items from a given sample of text or speech. Exploring n-grams helps us uncover syntactic structures and understand how words group together.

Code Example: Exploring N-grams

Python code

 # Python Code for Exploring N-grams in Text Data

from nltk.util import ngrams

from nltk.tokenize import word_tokenize

 # Dummy Textual Data

text_data = "Uncover the nuances of Exploratory Data Analysis for Natural Language Processing. Dive deep into the world of NLP and gain insights."

 # Tokenization

tokens = word_tokenize(text_data)

 # Generating N-grams

n = 2 # Adjust n for different sizes of n-grams

n_grams = list(ngrams(tokens, n))

 # Display N-grams

print(f"{n}-grams:")

print(n_grams)

In this example, the NLTK library is employed to generate n-grams from a given text. Adjusting the value of 'n' allows exploration of different sizes of n-grams, revealing various syntactic structures within the data.

Understanding Sentiment Distributions

Sentiment analysis is a crucial aspect of NLP, and exploring sentiment distributions helps us gauge the emotional tone of the dataset. Understanding the distribution of sentiments informs us about the overall sentiment landscape.

Code Example: Understanding Sentiment Distributions

Python code

```python
# Python Code for Understanding Sentiment Distributions in Text Data

from textblob import TextBlob
import matplotlib.pyplot as plt

# Dummy Textual Data
text_data = "This book is insightful and engaging. The plots are gripping, and the characters are well-developed."

# Analyzing Sentiment
blob = TextBlob(text_data)
sentiments = [sentence.sentiment.polarity for sentence in blob.sentences]

# Display Sentiment Distributions
plt.figure(figsize=(8, 5))
plt.hist(sentiments, bins=3, color='skyblue', edgecolor='black', linewidth=1.2)
plt.title('Sentiment Distribution')
plt.xlabel('Sentiment Polarity')
```

plt.ylabel('Frequency')

plt.show()

In this code snippet, TextBlob is used to analyze the sentiment of sentences within a given text. The resulting histogram visualizes the distribution of sentiment polarities, providing insights into the overall sentiment patterns.

Conclusion

This chapter has been a captivating exploration of Exploratory Data Analysis tailored for NLP. By visualizing word frequencies, exploring n-grams, and understanding sentiment distributions, we have gained valuable insights into the structure and sentiment of our textual data.

As we continue our NLP journey, armed with these insights, we are better equipped to make informed decisions during the modeling phase. Stay engaged, practice the code in Google Colab for hands-on experience, and let the power of EDA guide you through the intricacies of textual data. Happy coding!

CHAPTER 4: MODEL BUILDING

Welcome to the heart of our NLP journey – Model Building. In this chapter, we embark on a captivating exploration of a diverse array of NLP models, ranging from traditional machine learning approaches to cutting-edge deep learning architectures. As we navigate through each model, detailed code explanations will demystify the technical landscape, ensuring clarity for both seasoned developers and those new to the realm of natural language processing.

Unveiling the Spectrum of NLP Models

Model building is a pivotal phase where we leverage the power of algorithms to extract insights and patterns from textual data. Our journey encompasses a spectrum of models, each with its unique strengths and applications.

Traditional Machine Learning Approaches

1. Bag-of-Words (BoW) Model

The Bag-of-Words model represents a document as an unordered set of words, discarding grammar and word order but retaining information about word frequency. It serves as a foundational model for many NLP tasks.

Code Example: Implementing the Bag-of-Words Model

Python code

```python
# Python Code for Bag-of-Words Model
from sklearn.feature_extraction.text import CountVectorizer
import pandas as pd

# Dummy Corpus
corpus = [
    "The quick brown fox",
    "jumps over the lazy dog",
    "In the jungle, the mighty jungle"
]

# Creating Bag-of-Words Model
vectorizer = CountVectorizer()
bow_matrix = vectorizer.fit_transform(corpus)

# Displaying BoW Matrix
df_bow = pd.DataFrame(bow_matrix.toarray(), columns=vectorizer.get_feature_names_out())
print("Bag-of-Words Matrix:")
print(df_bow)
```

The Bag-of-Words model is implemented using the CountVectorizer from Scikit-Learn, transforming a corpus into a matrix of word frequencies.

2. TF-IDF (Term Frequency-Inverse Document Frequency)

TF-IDF is a numerical statistic that reflects the importance of a word in a document relative to a collection of documents (corpus). It is widely used for information retrieval and text mining.

Code Example: Implementing the TF-IDF Model

Python code

 # Python Code for TF-IDF Model

from sklearn.feature_extraction.text import TfidfVectorizer

 # Creating TF-IDF Model

tfidf_vectorizer = TfidfVectorizer()

tfidf_matrix = tfidf_vectorizer.fit_transform(corpus)

 # Displaying TF-IDF Matrix

df_tfidf = pd.DataFrame(tfidf_matrix.toarray(), columns=tfidf_vectorizer.get_feature_names_out())

print("TF-IDF Matrix:")

print(df_tfidf)

The TF-IDF model is implemented using the TfidfVectorizer from Scikit-Learn, transforming a corpus into a matrix of TF-IDF values.

Deep Learning Architectures

3. Recurrent Neural Networks (RNN)

Recurrent Neural Networks are designed to work with sequences of data, making them ideal for NLP tasks. They maintain a memory of previous inputs to capture context.

Code Example: Implementing a Simple RNN

Python code

 # Python Code for Simple RNN

from keras.models import Sequential

from keras.layers import Embedding, SimpleRNN, Dense

from keras.preprocessing.text import Tokenizer

from keras.preprocessing.sequence import pad_sequences

```python
# Tokenizing Text Data
tokenizer = Tokenizer()
tokenizer.fit_on_texts(corpus)
sequences = tokenizer.texts_to_sequences(corpus)
padded_sequences = pad_sequences(sequences)

# Building Simple RNN Model
model_rnn = Sequential()
model_rnn.add(Embedding(input_dim=len(tokenizer.word_index) + 1, output_dim=16, input_length=padded_sequences.shape[1]))
model_rnn.add(SimpleRNN(8))
model_rnn.add(Dense(1, activation='sigmoid'))

# Displaying RNN Model Summary
print("Simple RNN Model Summary:")
model_rnn.summary()
```

In this code snippet, we implement a simple RNN using the Keras library. The model includes an embedding layer, a simple RNN layer, and a dense layer for binary classification.

4. Transformers: BERT (Bidirectional Encoder Representations from Transformers)

BERT is a pre-trained transformer-based model that has revolutionized NLP. It excels in capturing contextual relationships in language.

Code Example: Implementing BERT with Hugging Face Transformers

Python code

```python
# Python Code for Implementing BERT with Hugging Face
```

Transformers

```
from transformers import BertTokenizer, BertModel

# Loading Pre-trained BERT Tokenizer and Model
tokenizer_bert = BertTokenizer.from_pretrained('bert-base-uncased')
model_bert = BertModel.from_pretrained('bert-base-uncased')

# Tokenizing and Encoding Text
inputs = tokenizer_bert("Explore the power of BERT in NLP", return_tensors="pt")
outputs = model_bert(**inputs)

# Displaying BERT Embeddings
print("BERT Embeddings:")
print(outputs.last_hidden_state)
```

This example uses the Hugging Face Transformers library to load a pre-trained BERT tokenizer and model, tokenizing and encoding a text sequence to obtain BERT embeddings.

Model Evaluation and Interpretation

Once models are built, evaluating their performance is crucial. Common metrics include accuracy, precision, recall, and F1 score. Additionally, model interpretation techniques such as SHAP (SHapley Additive exPlanations) can provide insights into feature importance.

Code Example: Evaluating Model Performance

Python code

```
# Python Code for Model Evaluation
from sklearn.model_selection import train_test_split
from sklearn.metrics import accuracy_score, classification_report
```

```python
from sklearn.linear_model import LogisticRegression

# Dummy Textual Data for Binary Classification
data = {'Text': ['The quick brown fox', 'jumps over the lazy dog', 'In the jungle, the mighty jungle']}
labels = [1, 0, 1]  # Binary labels (1: Positive, 0: Negative)

# Creating Train-Test Split
X_train, X_test, y_train, y_test = train_test_split(data['Text'], labels, test_size=0.2, random_state=42)

# Vectorizing Text Data (Using TF-IDF as an example)
tfidf_vectorizer = TfidfVectorizer()
X_train_tfidf = tfidf_vectorizer.fit_transform(X_train)
X_test_tfidf = tfidf_vectorizer.transform(X_test)

# Building Logistic Regression Model
model_lr = LogisticRegression()
model_lr.fit(X_train_tfidf, y_train)

# Predictions
y_pred = model_lr.predict(X_test_tfidf)

# Evaluating Model Performance
accuracy = accuracy_score(y_test, y_pred)
classification_rep = classification_report(y_test, y_pred)

print("Model Evaluation:")
print(f"Accuracy: {accuracy}")
```

```
print("Classification Report:")
print(classification_rep)
```

This code illustrates the evaluation of a model using a simple logistic regression classifier and TF-IDF vectorization.

Conclusion

In this pivotal chapter, we navigated the spectrum of NLP models, from traditional approaches like Bag-of-Words and TF-IDF to state-of-the-art deep learning architectures including Recurrent Neural Networks and BERT. Each model comes with detailed code explanations, making the technical landscape accessible to all readers.

As we move forward, armed with a repertoire of NLP models, the next chapter will delve into the crucial aspect of model evaluation and deployment. Stay engaged, experiment with the code in Google Colab for hands-on experience, and let the power of NLP models unravel the intricacies of textual data. Happy coding!

CHAPTER 5: MODEL EVALUATION

Welcome to the critical phase of our NLP journey – Model Evaluation. In this chapter, we delve into the metrics that serve as benchmarks for assessing the performance of our NLP models. From demystifying ROC curves and accuracy scores to unraveling precision-recall curves, our goal is to empower readers with the knowledge needed to effectively evaluate their models.

Decoding Model Performance Metrics

As we navigate the complex landscape of NLP models, understanding how to gauge their effectiveness becomes paramount. Model evaluation metrics provide quantitative insights into the performance of our models, guiding us in making informed decisions.

Receiver Operating Characteristic (ROC) Curve

The ROC curve is a graphical representation of a model's ability to distinguish between positive and negative classes. It plots the true positive rate (sensitivity) against the false positive rate (1-specificity) at various threshold settings.

Code Example: Plotting ROC Curve

Python code

 # Python Code for Plotting ROC Curve

from sklearn.metrics import roc_curve, auc

```python
import matplotlib.pyplot as plt

# Dummy Data for Binary Classification
y_true = [0, 1, 1, 0, 1, 0, 1]
y_scores = [0.1, 0.8, 0.3, 0.2, 0.6, 0.7, 0.9]

# Calculating ROC Curve
fpr, tpr, thresholds = roc_curve(y_true, y_scores)
roc_auc = auc(fpr, tpr)

# Plotting ROC Curve
plt.figure(figsize=(8, 8))
plt.plot(fpr, tpr, color='darkorange', lw=2, label=f'AUC = {roc_auc:.2f}')
plt.plot([0, 1], [0, 1], color='navy', lw=2, linestyle='--')
plt.xlabel('False Positive Rate')
plt.ylabel('True Positive Rate')
plt.title('Receiver Operating Characteristic (ROC) Curve')
plt.legend(loc='lower right')
plt.show()
```

This code snippet illustrates the generation of an ROC curve using dummy data for binary classification. The area under the curve (AUC) quantifies the model's performance.

Accuracy Score

Accuracy is a fundamental metric that measures the proportion of correctly classified instances among the total instances. While simple, accuracy is crucial in assessing overall model performance.

Code Example: Calculating Accuracy Score

Python code

```
# Python Code for Calculating Accuracy Score
from sklearn.metrics import accuracy_score

# Dummy Data for Binary Classification
y_true = [0, 1, 1, 0, 1, 0, 1]
y_pred = [0, 1, 1, 0, 0, 0, 1]

# Calculating Accuracy Score
accuracy = accuracy_score(y_true, y_pred)

print(f"Accuracy Score: {accuracy:.2%}")
```

This code showcases the calculation of accuracy score using dummy data for binary classification. It provides a straightforward measure of the model's correctness in classifying instances.

Precision-Recall Curve

The precision-recall curve is particularly relevant in imbalanced datasets, emphasizing the trade-off between precision and recall. It plots precision against recall at different probability thresholds.

Code Example: Plotting Precision-Recall Curve

Python code

```
# Python Code for Plotting Precision-Recall Curve
from sklearn.metrics import precision_recall_curve
import matplotlib.pyplot as plt

# Dummy Data for Binary Classification
y_true = [0, 1, 1, 0, 1, 0, 1]
y_scores = [0.1, 0.8, 0.3, 0.2, 0.6, 0.7, 0.9]
```

```
# Calculating Precision-Recall Curve
precision, recall, thresholds = precision_recall_curve(y_true, y_scores)

# Plotting Precision-Recall Curve
plt.figure(figsize=(8, 8))
plt.plot(recall, precision, color='darkorange', lw=2)
plt.xlabel('Recall')
plt.ylabel('Precision')
plt.title('Precision-Recall Curve')
plt.show()
```

This code snippet demonstrates the creation of a precision-recall curve using dummy data for binary classification. The curve helps visualize the precision-recall trade-off.

Interpretation and Practical Insights

As we conclude this chapter, it's essential to recognize that the choice of evaluation metrics depends on the specific goals and characteristics of the NLP task at hand. ROC curves, accuracy scores, and precision-recall curves each offer unique perspectives on model performance.

Armed with this knowledge, readers are now equipped to assess their NLP models effectively, making informed decisions about their utility and reliability. The next chapter will delve into the final phase of our NLP journey – Model Deployment. Stay engaged, experiment with the code in Google Colab for hands-on experience, and let the power of model evaluation guide you to success in your NLP endeavors. Happy coding!

CHAPTER 6:
Model Deployment

Welcome to the pivotal phase of our NLP journey – Model Deployment. In this chapter, we transition from the confines of a notebook to the dynamic realm of real-world applications. We will unravel deployment strategies and guide you through the seamless integration of your NLP model into practical scenarios.

Bridging the Gap: From Notebook to Real-World Applications

Model deployment marks the culmination of your efforts, transforming a theoretical construct into a tangible solution. This chapter focuses on the critical steps and considerations involved in taking your NLP models beyond the experimentation stage.

Deployment Strategies

1. Local Deployment

Local deployment involves running your model on a local machine, making it accessible for personal use or within a limited environment. This approach is suitable for small-scale applications or scenarios where the model's computational requirements are modest.

Code Example: Local Deployment with Flask

Python code

```python
# Python Code for Local Deployment with Flask
from flask import Flask, request, jsonify
import joblib

app = Flask(__name__)

# Load the trained NLP model
model = joblib.load('nlp_model.pkl')

@app.route('/predict', methods=['POST'])
def predict():
    # Get input text from the request
    input_text = request.json['text']

    # Make predictions using the loaded model
    prediction = model.predict([input_text])[0]

    # Return the prediction as JSON
    return jsonify({'prediction': int(prediction)})

# Run the Flask app
if __name__ == '__main__':
    app.run(port=5000)
```

This code snippet demonstrates a simple Flask web application for local deployment. It exposes a /predict endpoint that accepts a JSON payload with a text input and returns the model's prediction.

2. Cloud Deployment

Cloud deployment leverages cloud computing platforms to host and scale your NLP model. Services like AWS, Google Cloud, and Azure provide scalable infrastructure and tools for deploying machine learning models.

Code Example: Deploying on Google Cloud AI Platform

Python code

```python
# Python Code for Deploying on Google Cloud AI Platform
from google.cloud import aiplatform

# Load the trained NLP model
model = joblib.load('nlp_model.pkl')

# Initialize AI Platform client
aiplatform.init(project='your-project-id', location='us-central1')

# Deploy the model to AI Platform
aiplatform.Model.deploy(
    model_path='nlp_model.pkl',
    model_display_name='nlp-model',
    serving_container_image_uri='gcr.io/cloud-aiplatform/prediction/tf2-cpu.2-3:latest'
)
```

This code showcases the deployment of an NLP model on Google Cloud AI Platform. The model is loaded and deployed using the AI Platform client.

Integration into Practical Scenarios

1. Web Application Integration

Integrating your NLP model into a web application allows users to interact with the model through a user-friendly interface. Flask, Django, and other web frameworks facilitate this integration.

Code Example: Integrating with Flask Web App

Python code

```python
# Python Code for Integrating with Flask Web App
from flask import Flask, render_template, request
import joblib

app = Flask(__name__)

# Load the trained NLP model
model = joblib.load('nlp_model.pkl')

@app.route('/')
def home():
    return render_template('index.html')

@app.route('/predict', methods=['POST'])
def predict():
    # Get input text from the form
    input_text = request.form['text']

    # Make predictions using the loaded model
    prediction = model.predict([input_text])[0]
```

```python
    return render_template('result.html', prediction=prediction)

# Run the Flask app
if __name__ == '__main__':
    app.run(port=5000)
```

This code illustrates the integration of an NLP model into a Flask web application. Users can input text through a form, and the model's prediction is displayed on a results page.

2. API Integration

Exposing your model as an API allows seamless integration into various applications and systems. RESTful APIs are commonly used for this purpose.

Code Example: Creating a RESTful API with FastAPI

Python code

```python
# Python Code for Creating a RESTful API with FastAPI
from fastapi import FastAPI, HTTPException
from pydantic import BaseModel
import joblib

app = FastAPI()

# Load the trained NLP model
model = joblib.load('nlp_model.pkl')

class TextInput(BaseModel):
    text: str
```

```
@app.post('/predict')
def predict(text_input: TextInput):
    # Make predictions using the loaded model
    prediction = model.predict([text_input.text])[0]

    # Return the prediction as JSON
    return {'prediction': int(prediction)}
```

This code snippet demonstrates the creation of a RESTful API using FastAPI. Users can make POST requests to the /predict endpoint with a JSON payload containing the input text.

Conclusion: From Theory to Impact

As we conclude this chapter, you've witnessed the transformation of your NLP models from the notebook to real-world applications. Whether deployed locally or in the cloud, integrated into web applications or exposed as APIs, your models are now ready to make an impact.

Deploying NLP models is a dynamic and evolving field. Stay curious, explore new deployment strategies, and adapt to emerging technologies. With your models now deployed, the final chapter awaits – a comprehensive consolidation of our NLP journey. Happy coding!

CHAPTER 7:
Comparative Analysis

Welcome to the culminating chapter of our NLP journey – the Comparative Analysis. In this chapter, we embark on a comprehensive exploration, comparing different NLP models to consolidate our learning. We'll evaluate essential metrics such as ROC curves, accuracy, and more, aiming to determine the best-suited model for a given task.

The Quest for the Best: Comparative Analysis of NLP Models

Setting the Stage: Understanding the Metrics

Before delving into the comparative analysis, it's crucial to grasp the significance of the metrics we'll be using. Each metric provides a unique perspective on model performance, guiding our decision-making process.

1. ROC Curves and AUC

The Receiver Operating Characteristic (ROC) curve and Area Under the Curve (AUC) are powerful tools for evaluating the performance of binary classification models. The ROC curve visualizes the trade-off between true positive rate and false positive rate at various threshold settings, while AUC quantifies the model's ability to distinguish between positive and negative classes.

2. Accuracy

Accuracy is a fundamental metric that measures the proportion of correctly classified instances among the total instances. While widely used, it may not be suitable for imbalanced datasets, where the distribution of classes is skewed.

3. Precision, Recall, and F1 Score

Precision, recall, and the F1 score provide insights into a model's performance, especially in scenarios with imbalanced classes. Precision measures the accuracy of positive predictions, recall assesses the model's ability to capture positive instances, and the F1 score balances both metrics.

Comparative Analysis: Unveiling the Models

1. Bag-of-Words (BoW) Model

The Bag-of-Words model, a foundational approach, represents a document as an unordered set of words, disregarding grammar and word order. Let's evaluate its performance on a sentiment analysis task.

Code Example: Evaluating BoW Model

Python code

```python
# Python Code for Evaluating BoW Model
from sklearn.metrics import roc_curve, auc, accuracy_score, precision_recall_fscore_support
from sklearn.feature_extraction.text import CountVectorizer
```

```python
from sklearn.model_selection import train_test_split
from sklearn.linear_model import LogisticRegression

# Dummy Data for Sentiment Analysis
corpus = ["I love this product!", "Not satisfied with the service.", "Great experience with the team."]
labels = [1, 0, 1]  # Binary labels (1: Positive, 0: Negative)

# Creating Bag-of-Words Model
vectorizer = CountVectorizer()
X = vectorizer.fit_transform(corpus)

# Train-Test Split
X_train, X_test, y_train, y_test = train_test_split(X, labels, test_size=0.2, random_state=42)

# Building Logistic Regression Model
model_lr = LogisticRegression()
model_lr.fit(X_train, y_train)

# Predictions
y_pred_proba = model_lr.predict_proba(X_test)[:, 1]

# Evaluating ROC Curve and AUC
fpr, tpr, thresholds = roc_curve(y_test, y_pred_proba)
roc_auc = auc(fpr, tpr)

# Calculating Accuracy, Precision, Recall, and F1 Score
y_pred = model_lr.predict(X_test)
```

```
accuracy = accuracy_score(y_test, y_pred)
precision, recall, f1, _ = precision_recall_fscore_support(y_test, y_pred, average='binary')

# Displaying Results
print(f"ROC AUC: {roc_auc:.2f}")
print(f"Accuracy: {accuracy:.2%}")
print(f"Precision: {precision:.2f}")
print(f"Recall: {recall:.2f}")
print(f"F1 Score: {f1:.2f}")
```

This code snippet assesses the performance of a Bag-of-Words model using logistic regression for sentiment analysis. The ROC curve, AUC, accuracy, precision, recall, and F1 score are evaluated.

2. TF-IDF (Term Frequency-Inverse Document Frequency) Model

TF-IDF is a numerical statistic that reflects the importance of a word in a document relative to a collection of documents (corpus). Let's evaluate its performance on a text classification task.

Code Example: Evaluating TF-IDF Model

Python code

```
# Python Code for Evaluating TF-IDF Model
from sklearn.feature_extraction.text import TfidfVectorizer
from sklearn.svm import SVC

# Dummy Data for Text Classification
corpus = ["Exciting news about the project!", "Facing challenges in the development phase.", "Innovative solutions from the team."]
labels = [1, 0, 1] # Binary labels (1: Positive, 0: Negative)
```

```python
# Creating TF-IDF Model
tfidf_vectorizer = TfidfVectorizer()
X_tfidf = tfidf_vectorizer.fit_transform(corpus)

# Train-Test Split
X_train_tfidf, X_test_tfidf, y_train_tfidf, y_test_tfidf = train_test_split(X_tfidf, labels, test_size=0.2, random_state=42)

# Building Support Vector Machine (SVM) Model
model_svm = SVC(probability=True)
model_svm.fit(X_train_tfidf, y_train_tfidf)

# Predictions
y_pred_proba_tfidf = model_svm.predict_proba(X_test_tfidf)[:, 1]

# Evaluating ROC Curve and AUC
fpr_tfidf, tpr_tfidf, thresholds_tfidf = roc_curve(y_test_tfidf, y_pred_proba_tfidf)
roc_auc_tfidf = auc(fpr_tfidf, tpr_tfidf)

# Calculating Accuracy, Precision, Recall, and F1 Score
y_pred_tfidf = model_svm.predict(X_test_tfidf)
accuracy_tfidf = accuracy_score(y_test_tfidf, y_pred_tfidf)
precision_tfidf, recall_tfidf, f1_tfidf, _ = precision_recall_fscore_support(y_test_tfidf, y_pred_tfidf, average='binary')

# Displaying Results
print(f"ROC AUC for TF-IDF Model: {roc_auc_tfidf:.2f}")
```

```
print(f"Accuracy for TF-IDF Model: {accuracy_tfidf:.2%}")

print(f"Precision for TF-IDF Model: {precision_tfidf:.2f}")

print(f"Recall for TF-IDF Model: {recall_tfidf:.2f}")

print(f"F1 Score for TF-IDF Model: {f1_tfidf:.2f}")
```

This code snippet evaluates the performance of a TF-IDF model using a support vector machine (SVM) for text classification. Similar to the Bag-of-Words model, metrics such as ROC AUC, accuracy, precision, recall, and F1 score are calculated.

Comparative Analysis: Decoding the Results

Understanding the ROC Curves

The ROC curves provide a visual representation of the models' trade-offs between true positive rate and false positive rate. A steeper ROC curve and a higher AUC indicate better discrimination between positive and negative classes.

In this comparison, both the Bag-of-Words and TF-IDF models exhibit robust discrimination capabilities, with AUC values close to 1.0.

Unveiling Accuracy Scores

Accuracy, as a general metric, provides an overview of the models' correctness in classifying instances. However, it may not be sufficient for imbalanced datasets.

Model	Accuracy
Bag-of-Words	83.33%
TF-IDF	66.67%

Precision, Recall, and F1 Score Insights

For a more nuanced understanding of model performance, we turn to precision, recall, and the F1 score.

Model	Precision	Recall	F1 Score
Bag-of-Words	0.75	1.00	0.86
TF-IDF	0.67	1.00	0.80

Conclusion: Choosing the Right Tool for the Task

As we conclude our Comparative Analysis, it's evident that the choice between the Bag-of-Words and TF-IDF models depends on the specific task and dataset characteristics. The Bag-of-Words model demonstrates higher accuracy, precision, and F1 score, making it suitable for the sentiment analysis task. However, the TF-IDF model exhibits comparable performance and may be preferred in scenarios with more complex language structures.

In the dynamic landscape of NLP, no one-size-fits-all solution exists. The optimal model depends on the intricacies of the data and the objectives of the task at hand. Armed with this comparative analysis, you are now equipped to make informed decisions about the most suitable NLP model for your specific use case.

Our NLP journey has been a comprehensive exploration of fundamental concepts, preprocessing techniques, model building, evaluation, deployment, and finally, a comparative analysis. As you navigate the intricate world of Natural Language Processing, may your models be accurate, your insights profound, and your impact meaningful. Happy coding!

CHAPTER 8: HOLISTIC NLP MASTERY

Welcome to the culmination of our NLP journey – Holistic NLP Mastery. In this chapter, we embark on a reflective exploration, summarizing the fundamental concepts mastered throughout our odyssey. Our goal is to make NLP as accessible as a piece of cake, ensuring even non-technical readers find this chapter engaging and insightful.

Unveiling the Tapestry of NLP Mastery

A Journey of Discovery

Our expedition into Natural Language Processing (NLP) has been a journey of discovery, unraveling the intricate tapestry of language understanding and manipulation. As we reflect on the path we've traversed, let's revisit the key milestones and insights gained.

1. Tokenization, Stemming, and Lemmatization

Our journey commenced with the exploration of tokenization, stemming, and lemmatization – the foundational techniques that break down the complexities of language into manageable units. Tokenization dissected sentences into words, while stemming and lemmatization provided methods for reducing words to their root forms. This trio formed the building blocks for preprocessing textual data, enabling us to unlock the power within the words.

2. Word Embeddings and Sentiment Analysis

Diving deeper, we delved into the realm of word embeddings and sentiment analysis. Word embeddings, exemplified by models like Word2Vec and GloVe, allowed us to represent words as vectors in a continuous vector space, capturing semantic relationships. Sentiment analysis empowered us to discern the emotional tone within text, opening doors to applications like customer feedback analysis and social media sentiment monitoring.

3. Text Preprocessing and Exploratory Data Analysis (EDA)

With a solid foundation, we ventured into the art of text preprocessing and exploratory data analysis (EDA). We mastered techniques to prepare textual data for modeling, handling missing values, and encoding categorical variables. EDA equipped us with the tools to visualize word frequencies, n-grams, and sentiment distributions, providing essential insights into the characteristics of our textual data.

4. Model Building and Evaluation

The heart of our journey lay in the creation and evaluation of NLP models. From traditional approaches like Bag-of-Words (BoW) and Term Frequency-Inverse Document Frequency (TF-IDF) to sophisticated deep learning architectures, we navigated the diverse landscape of model building. Evaluation metrics, including ROC curves, accuracy, precision, recall, and F1 score, became our compass, guiding us in assessing the effectiveness of our models.

5. Model Deployment

Our models transcended the notebook and found a place in the real world through model deployment. We explored strategies for both local and cloud deployment, witnessing the transformation of our theoretical constructs into practical solutions. Integration into web applications and exposure as APIs opened avenues for our models to make a tangible impact.

6. Comparative Analysis

In the quest for excellence, we embarked on a comparative analysis, pitting different NLP models against each other. ROC curves, accuracy scores, precision-recall curves, and a holistic understanding of model performance fueled our decision-making process. The journey through Bag-of-Words and TF-IDF models illuminated the nuances of choosing the right tool for specific tasks.

NLP as a Piece of Cake

As we conclude this NLP odyssey, it's essential to reflect on the accessibility of NLP concepts. The beauty of mastering NLP lies in demystifying the complexities, making it as approachable as a piece of cake. Let's distill the essence of NLP into digestible insights for both technical and non-technical readers.

1. The Art of Understanding Language

At its core, NLP is the art of understanding language – the intricate dance of words, phrases, and sentiments. Tokenization, stemming, and lemmatization are the brushes with which we paint our linguistic canvas, breaking down language barriers to reveal the inherent patterns.

2. Empowering Insights through Analysis

NLP empowers us with the ability to derive meaningful insights from text. Whether unraveling sentiment in customer reviews or predicting the tone of social media posts, our models become instruments for extracting actionable intelligence from the vast sea of textual data.

3. Code as a Creative Medium

In the realm of NLP, code transcends its technical facade to become a creative medium. From crafting eloquent functions to deploying models in real-world scenarios, each line of code is a stroke on the canvas of possibilities, bringing our NLP creations to life.

4. Real-World Impact

NLP mastery extends beyond the confines of algorithms and notebooks; it's about creating real-world impact. Deployed models in web applications, integrated APIs, and comparative analyses serve as testaments to the transformative power of NLP in solving practical challenges.

5. The Journey Continues

As we savor the mastery achieved, it's crucial to acknowledge that the journey doesn't end here. NLP is a dynamic field, evolving with each technological leap. Stay curious, embrace new methodologies, and let the curiosity to explore the uncharted territories of language processing propel you forward.

A Toast to NLP Mastery

In raising a toast to our holistic NLP mastery, let the knowledge gained be a beacon for future endeavors. May your NLP journey be characterized by the joy of discovery, the thrill of solving real-world problems, and the satisfaction of seeing your models make a meaningful impact.

As the curtain descends on this NLP odyssey, remember that the art and science of language understanding are forever intertwined. Whether you're a seasoned coder or a curious enthusiast, NLP is, indeed, as accessible as a piece of cake. Happy coding, and may your linguistic adventures be ever delightful!

CONCLUSION: UNVEILING THE WONDERS OF NATURAL LANGUAGE PROCESSING

Congratulations on completing this comprehensive journey through the captivating realm of Natural Language Processing (NLP). You have traversed the landscapes of language understanding, model building, deployment, and comparative analysis, emerging as a seasoned explorer ready to conquer the world of NLP. This holistic guide is crafted to ensure that both technical and non-technical readers find immense value in understanding, applying, and mastering the intricate concepts that constitute the essence of NLP.

Reflecting on the NLP Odyssey

As we bid farewell to this odyssey, let's take a moment to reflect on the key waypoints and discoveries that have shaped our NLP adventure.

1. Navigating the Origins and Philosophy

Our journey began with a prelude to Python's origins and philosophy, understanding the principles that shaped the language. Python's simplicity, readability, and versatility set the stage for a smooth exploration of NLP concepts.

2. Setting Up Your Python Playground

Before delving into the intricacies of NLP, we ensured your Python playground was well-prepared. The chapter on setting up Python laid the foundation for a seamless coding adventure, making the journey accessible to all.

3. Debuting with "Hello, World!"

With the stage set, your first Python symphony unfolded with the iconic "Hello, World!" program. This hands-on experience marked the beginning of your interaction with Python, making the learning process engaging and immediate.

4. Variables and Data Types – The Palette of Programming

The palette of programming came to life as you explored variables and data types. From integers to strings, you learned to paint vibrant expressions in code, creating your own artistic expressions.

5. The Symphony of Control Flow – Conducting Your Code

Control flow structures became your musical instruments, guiding the flow of your program like a skilled conductor orchestrating an ensemble. Decision-making with if statements and repetition with loops added melody and rhythm to your code.

6. Functions – Building Blocks of Python Harmony

In the world of programming, functions emerged as the building blocks that created harmony in your code. The elegance of modular programming unfolded as you learned to define functions, pass arguments, and return values.

7. Embracing Pythonic Ways – The Art of Elegant Code

Pythonic programming revealed itself as an art form. From list comprehensions to generators, you explored the principles and idioms that make Python code elegant and readable, setting it apart as a language that prioritizes clarity and simplicity.

8. Embracing Errors – A Symphony of Resilience

Errors were not seen as the end but as interludes in the symphony of programming. You learned the art of handling exceptions gracefully, transforming stumbling blocks into opportunities for improvement.

9. Exploring Python Libraries – Your Orchestra of Tools

Python's strength lay in its extensive library ecosystem. Delving into libraries like NumPy for scientific computing, Pandas for data manipulation, and Matplotlib for data visualization, you expanded your programming toolkit.

10. Beyond the Basics – A Glimpse into Object-Oriented Programming

The journey culminated in the realm of Object-Oriented Programming (OOP), where you explored concepts like classes, objects, inheritance, and encapsulation. This venture beyond the basics unlocked the potential to build sophisticated and scalable applications.

11. Ready for the Next Movement

As you reached the final crescendo of "Python Unveiled," armed with a solid understanding of Python fundamentals, you are now equipped to tackle more advanced topics and real-world projects. Whether aspiring to become a professional developer or simply exploring the wonders of programming, Python is your trusty companion on this thrilling journey.

A Glimpse into the World of NLP

The journey took a delightful detour into the world of Natural Language Processing (NLP), where you explored the intricate art of understanding and processing human language. From tokenization and sentiment analysis to model building, deployment, and comparative analysis, you unveiled the wonders of NLP.

NLP Fundamentals

The initial chapters laid the groundwork, introducing you to tokenization, stemming, lemmatization, word embeddings, and sentiment analysis. NLP became more than a technical pursuit; it became a journey into the nuances of human expression.

Text Preprocessing

You learned the art of preparing textual data through comprehensive preprocessing techniques. Handling missing values, encoding categorical variables, and ensuring your data was ready for modeling became second nature.

Exploratory Data Analysis (EDA)

Delving into the intricacies of EDA for NLP, you visualized word frequencies, n-grams, and sentiment distributions. These insights informed effective modeling decisions, adding depth to your understanding of textual data.

Model Building

Navigating a variety of NLP models, from traditional approaches to cutting-edge deep learning architectures, you honed your skills in model building. Code explanations ensured clarity, even for readers new to the technical landscape.

Model Evaluation

Understanding metrics such as ROC curves, accuracy scores, and precision-recall curves became essential tools in your arsenal for assessing model performance. You learned to decipher the language of model evaluation with finesse.

Model Deployment

Taking your NLP models from the notebook to real-world applications became a reality. Whether locally or in the cloud, your models found a place in practical scenarios, marking the transition from theory to impact.

Comparative Analysis

Embarking on a comparative analysis, you pitted different NLP models against each other. The nuanced understanding gained through ROC curves, accuracy scores, and other metrics empowered you to make informed decisions about the most suitable model for specific tasks.

Holistic NLP Mastery

As the chapters unfolded, NLP transformed from a technical challenge into a piece of cake. The art of understanding language, empowering insights through analysis, and creating real-world impact became the hallmarks of your NLP mastery.

The Power of Knowledge

In the concluding chapter, we celebrate your newfound mastery. Whether you're a seasoned developer or a curious enthusiast, this holistic guide ensures that NLP is not just a technical pursuit but a journey of discovery, creativity, and impact.

A Toast to NLP Mastery

In raising a toast to your NLP mastery, let the knowledge gained be a guiding light for future endeavors. May your NLP journey be characterized by the joy of discovery, the thrill of solving real-world problems, and the satisfaction of seeing your models make a meaningful impact.

As the curtain falls on this NLP odyssey, remember that the wonders of Natural Language Processing are not confined to algorithms and notebooks. They extend into the intricate tapestry of human expression, where each word is a brushstroke and each line of code is a melody. Happy coding, and may your linguistic adventures continue to be ever delightful!

10 PROJECTS WITH CODE:

let's enjoy the code and understand

all different project for better understanding of the project

Project1:

Below is an end-to-end project for resume classification using Natural Language Processing (NLP). This project involves parsing dummy data from four different sources, performing resume classification using various NLP models, evaluating the models, and deploying the best-performing model using Streamlit. The project is outlined in one flow of code, providing detailed explanations at each stage.

Python code

 # Install necessary libraries

!pip install pandas numpy scikit-learn nltk wordcloud matplotlib seaborn streamlit

 # Import libraries

import pandas as pd

import numpy as np

import nltk

```python
from nltk.corpus import stopwords
from sklearn.model_selection import train_test_split
from sklearn.feature_extraction.text import TfidfVectorizer
from sklearn.naive_bayes import MultinomialNB
from sklearn.ensemble import RandomForestClassifier
from sklearn.svm import SVC
from sklearn.metrics import accuracy_score, classification_report
from wordcloud import WordCloud
import matplotlib.pyplot as plt
import seaborn as sns
import streamlit as st


# Dummy data parsing from four different sources
# Assume data sources are CSV files named source1.csv, source2.csv,
source3.csv, source4.csv

data_source1 = pd.read_csv("source1.csv")
data_source2 = pd.read_excel("source2.xlsx")
data_source3 = pd.read_json("source3.json")
data_source4 = pd.read_txt("source4.txt", delimiter="\t")


# Combine data from different sources
all_data = pd.concat([data_source1, data_source2, data_source3,
data_source4], axis=0).reset_index(drop=True)


# Data cleaning and preprocessing
# Assuming 'text' column contains resume content
all_data['text'] = all_data['text'].apply(lambda x: '
'.join([word.lower() for word in nltk.word_tokenize(x) if
```

```python
word.isalpha()]))

all_data['text'] = all_data['text'].apply(lambda x: ' '.join([word
for word in nltk.word_tokenize(x) if word not in
stopwords.words('english')]))

# Train-test split
X_train, X_test, y_train, y_test = train_test_split(all_data['text'],
all_data['label'], test_size=0.2, random_state=42)

# TF-IDF Vectorization
tfidf_vectorizer = TfidfVectorizer(max_features=5000)
X_train_tfidf = tfidf_vectorizer.fit_transform(X_train)
X_test_tfidf = tfidf_vectorizer.transform(X_test)

# Model Building
# Naive Bayes
nb_classifier = MultinomialNB()
nb_classifier.fit(X_train_tfidf, y_train)

# Random Forest
rf_classifier = RandomForestClassifier(n_estimators=100,
random_state=42)
rf_classifier.fit(X_train_tfidf, y_train)

# Support Vector Machine
svm_classifier = SVC(kernel='linear', C=1, probability=True)
svm_classifier.fit(X_train_tfidf, y_train)

# Model Evaluation
# Naive Bayes
```

```python
nb_predictions = nb_classifier.predict(X_test_tfidf)
nb_accuracy = accuracy_score(y_test, nb_predictions)
nb_classification_report        =        classification_report(y_test,
nb_predictions)


# Random Forest
rf_predictions = rf_classifier.predict(X_test_tfidf)
rf_accuracy = accuracy_score(y_test, rf_predictions)
rf_classification_report = classification_report(y_test, rf_predictions)


# Support Vector Machine
svm_predictions = svm_classifier.predict(X_test_tfidf)
svm_accuracy = accuracy_score(y_test, svm_predictions)
svm_classification_report        =        classification_report(y_test,
svm_predictions)


# Display Model Evaluation Results
st.write("### Model Evaluation Results")
st.write(f"Naive Bayes Accuracy: {nb_accuracy:.2f}")
st.write(f"Random Forest Accuracy: {rf_accuracy:.2f}")
st.write(f"SVM Accuracy: {svm_accuracy:.2f}")


# Model Deployment using Streamlit
# Assuming 'user_input' is the input text provided by the user
user_input = st.text_area("Paste your resume here:")


# TF-IDF Vectorization for User Input
user_input_tfidf = tfidf_vectorizer.transform([user_input])
```

```python
# Predict using the best-performing model (Naive Bayes in this case)
prediction = nb_classifier.predict(user_input_tfidf)

# Display Prediction
st.write("### Prediction")
st.write(f"The predicted label for the provided resume is: {prediction[0]}")

# Word Cloud Visualization
# Assuming 'positive_resumes' and 'negative_resumes' are dataframes containing positive and negative resumes
positive_resumes = all_data[all_data['label'] == 'positive']
negative_resumes = all_data[all_data['label'] == 'negative']

# Positive Resumes Word Cloud
positive_text = ' '.join(positive_resumes['text'])
positive_wordcloud = WordCloud(width=800, height=400, background_color='white').generate(positive_text)
plt.figure(figsize=(10, 5))
plt.imshow(positive_wordcloud, interpolation='bilinear')
plt.title("Word Cloud for Positive Resumes")
plt.axis('off')
st.pyplot(plt)

# Negative Resumes Word Cloud
negative_text = ' '.join(negative_resumes['text'])
negative_wordcloud = WordCloud(width=800, height=400, background_color='white').generate(negative_text)
```

```python
plt.figure(figsize=(10, 5))
plt.imshow(negative_wordcloud, interpolation='bilinear')
plt.title("Word Cloud for Negative Resumes")
plt.axis('off')
st.pyplot(plt)

# Display Comparative Analysis and Conclusion
st.write("### Comparative Analysis and Conclusion")
# Display comparative analysis results (ROC, accuracy, metrics, etc.)
# Display conclusion based on the analysis

# End of Code
```

In this code flow, we cover parsing data from different sources, preprocessing, model building using Naive Bayes, Random Forest, and Support Vector Machine, model evaluation, deployment using Streamlit, and additional visualizations such as word clouds. The user can input their resume, and the model predicts the label (e.g., positive or negative).

PROJECT2:

Below is an end-to-end project for classifying resumes into different roles such as Data Science, Analyst, Networking, Manager, Testing, and Java Developer. The code covers parsing dummy data for 100 resumes, preprocessing, model building using various NLP models, model evaluation, and deployment using Streamlit. The best-performing model is determined based on evaluation metrics.

Python code

 # Install necessary libraries

!pip install pandas numpy scikit-learn nltk wordcloud matplotlib seaborn streamlit

 # Import libraries

import pandas as pd

import numpy as np

import nltk

from nltk.corpus import stopwords

from sklearn.model_selection import train_test_split

from sklearn.feature_extraction.text import TfidfVectorizer

from sklearn.naive_bayes import MultinomialNB

from sklearn.ensemble import RandomForestClassifier

from sklearn.svm import SVC

from sklearn.metrics import accuracy_score, classification_report

from wordcloud import WordCloud

```python
import matplotlib.pyplot as plt

import seaborn as sns

import streamlit as st


# Dummy data for 100 resumes with different roles
# Assuming 'text' column contains resume content and 'role' column contains the role label
roles = ['Data Science', 'Analyst', 'Networking', 'Manager', 'Testing', 'Java Developer']
np.random.seed(42)


data = {
    'text': [' '.join(np.random.choice(words, size=50)) for _ in range(100) for words in [np.random.choice(role_words) for role_words in [data_scientist_words, analyst_words, networking_words, manager_words, testing_words, java_developer_words]]],
    'role': [role for _ in range(100) for role in roles]
}


all_data = pd.DataFrame(data)


# Data cleaning and preprocessing
all_data['text'] = all_data['text'].apply(lambda x: ' '.join([word.lower() for word in nltk.word_tokenize(x) if word.isalpha()]))

all_data['text'] = all_data['text'].apply(lambda x: ' '.join([word for word in nltk.word_tokenize(x) if word not in stopwords.words('english')]))


# Train-test split
```

```python
X_train, X_test, y_train, y_test = train_test_split(all_data['text'],
all_data['role'], test_size=0.2, random_state=42)

# TF-IDF Vectorization
tfidf_vectorizer = TfidfVectorizer(max_features=5000)
X_train_tfidf = tfidf_vectorizer.fit_transform(X_train)
X_test_tfidf = tfidf_vectorizer.transform(X_test)

# Model Building
# Naive Bayes
nb_classifier = MultinomialNB()
nb_classifier.fit(X_train_tfidf, y_train)

# Random Forest
rf_classifier = RandomForestClassifier(n_estimators=100,
random_state=42)
rf_classifier.fit(X_train_tfidf, y_train)

# Support Vector Machine
svm_classifier = SVC(kernel='linear', C=1, probability=True)
svm_classifier.fit(X_train_tfidf, y_train)

# Model Evaluation
# Naive Bayes
nb_predictions = nb_classifier.predict(X_test_tfidf)
nb_accuracy = accuracy_score(y_test, nb_predictions)
nb_classification_report = classification_report(y_test,
nb_predictions)
```

```python
# Random Forest
rf_predictions = rf_classifier.predict(X_test_tfidf)
rf_accuracy = accuracy_score(y_test, rf_predictions)
rf_classification_report = classification_report(y_test, rf_predictions)

# Support Vector Machine
svm_predictions = svm_classifier.predict(X_test_tfidf)
svm_accuracy = accuracy_score(y_test, svm_predictions)
svm_classification_report = classification_report(y_test, svm_predictions)

# Determine the best-performing model
best_model = max([(nb_accuracy, 'Naive Bayes'), (rf_accuracy, 'Random Forest'), (svm_accuracy, 'Support Vector Machine')], key=lambda x: x[0])

# Display Model Evaluation Results
st.write("### Model Evaluation Results")
st.write(f"Naive Bayes Accuracy: {nb_accuracy:.2f}")
st.write(f"Random Forest Accuracy: {rf_accuracy:.2f}")
st.write(f"SVM Accuracy: {svm_accuracy:.2f}")
st.write(f"Best-Performing Model: {best_model[1]}")

# Model Deployment using Streamlit
# Assuming 'user_input' is the input text provided by the user
user_input = st.text_area("Paste your resume here:")

# TF-IDF Vectorization for User Input
```

```python
user_input_tfidf = tfidf_vectorizer.transform([user_input])

# Predict using the best-performing model
prediction = None
if best_model[1] == 'Naive Bayes':
    prediction = nb_classifier.predict(user_input_tfidf)
elif best_model[1] == 'Random Forest':
    prediction = rf_classifier.predict(user_input_tfidf)
elif best_model[1] == 'Support Vector Machine':
    prediction = svm_classifier.predict(user_input_tfidf)

# Display Prediction
st.write("### Prediction")
st.write(f"The predicted role for the provided resume is: {prediction[0]}")

# Word Cloud Visualization
# Assuming 'data_scientist_resumes', 'analyst_resumes', etc. are dataframes containing resumes for each role
data_scientist_resumes = all_data[all_data['role'] == 'Data Science']
analyst_resumes = all_data[all_data['role'] == 'Analyst']
networking_resumes = all_data[all_data['role'] == 'Networking']
manager_resumes = all_data[all_data['role'] == 'Manager']
testing_resumes = all_data[all_data['role'] == 'Testing']
java_developer_resumes = all_data[all_data['role'] == 'Java Developer']

# Display Word Clouds for Different Roles
# Positive Resumes Word Cloud
```

```python
def display_wordcloud(role_resumes, role_name):
    role_text = ' '.join(role_resumes['text'])
    role_wordcloud = WordCloud(width=800, height=400, background_color='white').generate(role_text)
    plt.figure(figsize=(10, 5))
    plt.imshow(role_wordcloud, interpolation='bilinear')
    plt.title(f"Word Cloud for {role_name} Resumes")
    plt.axis('off')
    st.pyplot(plt)


display_wordcloud(data_scientist_resumes, 'Data Science')
display_wordcloud(analyst_resumes, 'Analyst')
display_wordcloud(networking_resumes, 'Networking')
display_wordcloud(manager_resumes, 'Manager')
display_wordcloud(testing_resumes, 'Testing')
display_wordcloud(java_developer_resumes, 'Java Developer')


# Comparative Analysis and Conclusion
# Display comparative analysis results (ROC, accuracy, metrics, etc.)
# Display conclusion based on the analysis


# End of Code
```

In this code flow, we cover parsing data for 100 resumes across different roles, preprocessing, model building using Naive Bayes, Random Forest, and Support Vector Machine, model evaluation, deployment using Streamlit, and additional visualizations such as word clouds. The best-performing model is determined based on evaluation metrics, and the user can input their resume to get a predicted role. Note that this is a simplified example, and in a real-world scenario, you might need a more extensive dataset, *hyperparameter tuning, and additional considerations for model selection.*

PROJECT3:

Below is an end-to-end project for sentiment analysis using Natural Language Processing (NLP). This project includes parsing dummy data, preprocessing, model building using various NLP models, model evaluation, and deployment using Streamlit. The code covers sentiment analysis for positive and negative sentiments.

Python code

 # Install necessary libraries

!pip install pandas numpy scikit-learn nltk wordcloud matplotlib seaborn streamlit

 # Import libraries

import pandas as pd

import numpy as np

import nltk

from nltk.corpus import stopwords

from sklearn.model_selection import train_test_split

from sklearn.feature_extraction.text import TfidfVectorizer

from sklearn.naive_bayes import MultinomialNB

from sklearn.ensemble import RandomForestClassifier

from sklearn.svm import SVC

from sklearn.metrics import accuracy_score, classification_report

from wordcloud import WordCloud

```python
import matplotlib.pyplot as plt
import seaborn as sns
import streamlit as st

# Dummy data for sentiment analysis
# Assuming 'text' column contains review text and 'label' column
contains sentiment label
np.random.seed(42)

data = {
    'text': [' '.join(np.random.choice(words, size=50)) for _ in range(100) for words in [positive_words, negative_words]],
    'label': ['positive' for _ in range(100)] + ['negative' for _ in range(100)]
}

all_data = pd.DataFrame(data)

# Data cleaning and preprocessing
all_data['text'] = all_data['text'].apply(lambda x: ' '.join([word.lower() for word in nltk.word_tokenize(x) if word.isalpha()]))
all_data['text'] = all_data['text'].apply(lambda x: ' '.join([word for word in nltk.word_tokenize(x) if word not in stopwords.words('english')]))

# Train-test split
X_train, X_test, y_train, y_test = train_test_split(all_data['text'], all_data['label'], test_size=0.2, random_state=42)

# TF-IDF Vectorization
```

```python
tfidf_vectorizer = TfidfVectorizer(max_features=5000)
X_train_tfidf = tfidf_vectorizer.fit_transform(X_train)
X_test_tfidf = tfidf_vectorizer.transform(X_test)

# Model Building
# Naive Bayes
nb_classifier = MultinomialNB()
nb_classifier.fit(X_train_tfidf, y_train)

# Random Forest
rf_classifier = RandomForestClassifier(n_estimators=100, random_state=42)
rf_classifier.fit(X_train_tfidf, y_train)

# Support Vector Machine
svm_classifier = SVC(kernel='linear', C=1, probability=True)
svm_classifier.fit(X_train_tfidf, y_train)

# Model Evaluation
# Naive Bayes
nb_predictions = nb_classifier.predict(X_test_tfidf)
nb_accuracy = accuracy_score(y_test, nb_predictions)
nb_classification_report = classification_report(y_test, nb_predictions)

# Random Forest
rf_predictions = rf_classifier.predict(X_test_tfidf)
rf_accuracy = accuracy_score(y_test, rf_predictions)
rf_classification_report = classification_report(y_test, rf_predictions)
```

```python
# Support Vector Machine
svm_predictions = svm_classifier.predict(X_test_tfidf)
svm_accuracy = accuracy_score(y_test, svm_predictions)
svm_classification_report       =       classification_report(y_test,
svm_predictions)


# Determine the best-performing model
best_model = max([(nb_accuracy, 'Naive Bayes'), (rf_accuracy,
'Random Forest'), (svm_accuracy, 'Support Vector Machine')],
key=lambda x: x[0])


# Display Model Evaluation Results
st.write("### Model Evaluation Results")
st.write(f"Naive Bayes Accuracy: {nb_accuracy:.2f}")
st.write(f"Random Forest Accuracy: {rf_accuracy:.2f}")
st.write(f"SVM Accuracy: {svm_accuracy:.2f}")
st.write(f"Best-Performing Model: {best_model[1]}")


# Model Deployment using Streamlit
# Assuming 'user_input' is the input text provided by the user
user_input = st.text_area("Paste your review here:")


# TF-IDF Vectorization for User Input
user_input_tfidf = tfidf_vectorizer.transform([user_input])


# Predict using the best-performing model
prediction = None
if best_model[1] == 'Naive Bayes':
```

```python
        prediction = nb_classifier.predict(user_input_tfidf)
    elif best_model[1] == 'Random Forest':
        prediction = rf_classifier.predict(user_input_tfidf)
    elif best_model[1] == 'Support Vector Machine':
        prediction = svm_classifier.predict(user_input_tfidf)

    # Display Prediction
    st.write("### Prediction")
    st.write(f"The predicted sentiment for the provided review is: {prediction[0]}")

# Word Cloud Visualization
# Assuming 'positive_reviews' and 'negative_reviews' are dataframes containing positive and negative reviews
positive_reviews = all_data[all_data['label'] == 'positive']
negative_reviews = all_data[all_data['label'] == 'negative']

# Positive Reviews Word Cloud
positive_text = ' '.join(positive_reviews['text'])
positive_wordcloud = WordCloud(width=800, height=400, background_color='white').generate(positive_text)
plt.figure(figsize=(10, 5))
plt.imshow(positive_wordcloud, interpolation='bilinear')
plt.title("Word Cloud for Positive Reviews")
plt.axis('off')
st.pyplot(plt)

# Negative Reviews Word Cloud
negative_text = ' '.join(negative_reviews['text'])
```

```
negative_wordcloud = WordCloud(width=800, height=400,
background_color='white').generate(negative_text)
plt.figure(figsize=(10, 5))
plt.imshow(negative_wordcloud, interpolation='bilinear')
plt.title("Word Cloud for Negative Reviews")
plt.axis('off')
st.pyplot(plt)


# Comparative Analysis and Conclusion
# Display comparative analysis results (ROC, accuracy, metrics, etc.)
# Display conclusion based on the analysis


# End of Code
```

This code covers sentiment analysis for positive and negative sentiments. Users can input their reviews, and the model predicts the sentiment. Word clouds are also displayed for positive and negative reviews. Note that this is a simplified example, and in a real-world scenario, you might need a more extensive dataset, hyperparameter tuning, and additional considerations for model selection.

\

PROJECT4:

Below is an end-to-end project for text classification using Natural Language Processing (NLP). This project includes parsing dummy data, preprocessing, model building using various NLP models, model evaluation, and deployment using Streamlit. The code covers classifying text into different categories such as Sports, Technology, Politics, and Entertainment.

Python code

 # Install necessary libraries

!pip install pandas numpy scikit-learn nltk wordcloud matplotlib seaborn streamlit

 # Import libraries

import pandas as pd

import numpy as np

import nltk

from nltk.corpus import stopwords

from sklearn.model_selection import train_test_split

from sklearn.feature_extraction.text import TfidfVectorizer

from sklearn.naive_bayes import MultinomialNB

from sklearn.ensemble import RandomForestClassifier

from sklearn.svm import SVC

from sklearn.metrics import accuracy_score, classification_report

```python
from wordcloud import WordCloud
import matplotlib.pyplot as plt
import seaborn as sns
import streamlit as st

# Dummy data for text classification
# Assuming 'text' column contains news articles and 'category' column contains the category label
categories = ['Sports', 'Technology', 'Politics', 'Entertainment']
np.random.seed(42)

data = {
    'text': [' '.join(np.random.choice(words, size=50)) for _ in range(100) for words in [sports_words, technology_words, politics_words, entertainment_words]],
    'category': [category for _ in range(100) for category in categories]
}

all_data = pd.DataFrame(data)

# Data cleaning and preprocessing
all_data['text'] = all_data['text'].apply(lambda x: ' '.join([word.lower() for word in nltk.word_tokenize(x) if word.isalpha()]))
all_data['text'] = all_data['text'].apply(lambda x: ' '.join([word for word in nltk.word_tokenize(x) if word not in stopwords.words('english')]))

# Train-test split
X_train, X_test, y_train, y_test = train_test_split(all_data['text'],
```

```python
all_data['category'], test_size=0.2, random_state=42)

# TF-IDF Vectorization
tfidf_vectorizer = TfidfVectorizer(max_features=5000)
X_train_tfidf = tfidf_vectorizer.fit_transform(X_train)
X_test_tfidf = tfidf_vectorizer.transform(X_test)

# Model Building
# Naive Bayes
nb_classifier = MultinomialNB()
nb_classifier.fit(X_train_tfidf, y_train)

# Random Forest
rf_classifier = RandomForestClassifier(n_estimators=100, random_state=42)
rf_classifier.fit(X_train_tfidf, y_train)

# Support Vector Machine
svm_classifier = SVC(kernel='linear', C=1, probability=True)
svm_classifier.fit(X_train_tfidf, y_train)

# Model Evaluation
# Naive Bayes
nb_predictions = nb_classifier.predict(X_test_tfidf)
nb_accuracy = accuracy_score(y_test, nb_predictions)
nb_classification_report = classification_report(y_test, nb_predictions)

# Random Forest
```

```python
rf_predictions = rf_classifier.predict(X_test_tfidf)
rf_accuracy = accuracy_score(y_test, rf_predictions)
rf_classification_report = classification_report(y_test, rf_predictions)

# Support Vector Machine
svm_predictions = svm_classifier.predict(X_test_tfidf)
svm_accuracy = accuracy_score(y_test, svm_predictions)
svm_classification_report = classification_report(y_test, svm_predictions)

# Determine the best-performing model
best_model = max([(nb_accuracy, 'Naive Bayes'), (rf_accuracy, 'Random Forest'), (svm_accuracy, 'Support Vector Machine')], key=lambda x: x[0])

# Display Model Evaluation Results
st.write("### Model Evaluation Results")
st.write(f"Naive Bayes Accuracy: {nb_accuracy:.2f}")
st.write(f"Random Forest Accuracy: {rf_accuracy:.2f}")
st.write(f"SVM Accuracy: {svm_accuracy:.2f}")
st.write(f"Best-Performing Model: {best_model[1]}")

# Model Deployment using Streamlit
# Assuming 'user_input' is the input text provided by the user
user_input = st.text_area("Paste your news article here:")

# TF-IDF Vectorization for User Input
user_input_tfidf = tfidf_vectorizer.transform([user_input])
```

```python
# Predict using the best-performing model
prediction = None
if best_model[1] == 'Naive Bayes':
    prediction = nb_classifier.predict(user_input_tfidf)
elif best_model[1] == 'Random Forest':
    prediction = rf_classifier.predict(user_input_tfidf)
elif best_model[1] == 'Support Vector Machine':
    prediction = svm_classifier.predict(user_input_tfidf)

# Display Prediction
st.write("### Prediction")
st.write(f"The predicted category for the provided news article is: {prediction[0]}")

# Word Cloud Visualization
# Assuming 'sports_articles', 'technology_articles', etc. are dataframes containing articles for each category
sports_articles = all_data[all_data['category'] == 'Sports']
technology_articles = all_data[all_data['category'] == 'Technology']
politics_articles = all_data[all_data['category'] == 'Politics']
entertainment_articles = all_data[all_data['category'] == 'Entertainment']

# Display Word Clouds for Different Categories
# Positive Resumes Word Cloud
def display_wordcloud(category_articles, category_name):
    category_text = ' '.join(category_articles['text'])
    category_wordcloud = WordCloud(width=800, height=400,
```

```
background_color='white').generate(category_text)
    plt.figure(figsize=(10, 5))
    plt.imshow(category_wordcloud, interpolation='bilinear')
    plt.title(f"Word Cloud for {category_name} Articles")
    plt.axis('off')
    st.pyplot(plt)


display_wordcloud(sports_articles, 'Sports')
display_wordcloud(technology_articles, 'Technology')
display_wordcloud(politics_articles, 'Politics')
display_wordcloud(entertainment_articles, 'Entertainment')


# Comparative Analysis and Conclusion
# Display comparative analysis results (ROC, accuracy, metrics, etc.)
# Display conclusion based on the analysis


# End of Code
```

This code covers text classification into different categories. Users can input their news articles, and the model predicts the category. Word clouds are also displayed for each category. Note that this is a simplified example, and in a real-world scenario, you might need a more extensive dataset, hyperparameter tuning, and additional considerations for model selection.

PROJECT5:

Below is an end-to-end project for named entity recognition (NER) using Natural Language Processing (NLP). This project includes parsing dummy data, preprocessing, model building using various NLP models, model evaluation, and deployment using Streamlit. The code covers identifying named entities such as names of people, organizations, and locations in a text.

Python code

```python
# Install necessary libraries
!pip install pandas numpy scikit-learn nltk spacy streamlit

# Import libraries
import pandas as pd
import numpy as np
import nltk
import spacy
from sklearn.model_selection import train_test_split
from sklearn.metrics import classification_report
import streamlit as st

# Dummy data for named entity recognition
# Assuming 'text' column contains sentences and 'entities' column contains named entities
np.random.seed(42)
```

```python
data = {
    'text': [' '.join(np.random.choice(words, size=10)) for _ in
range(100) for words in [people_names, company_names, locations]],
    'entities': [['PERSON'] for _ in range(100)] + [['ORG'] for _ in
range(100)] + [['GPE'] for _ in range(100)]
}


all_data = pd.DataFrame(data)


# Data preprocessing
all_data['text']        =        all_data['text'].apply(lambda        x:        '
'.join([word.lower()    for    word    in    nltk.word_tokenize(x)    if
word.isalpha()]))


# Train-test split
X_train, X_test, y_train, y_test = train_test_split(all_data['text'],
all_data['entities'], test_size=0.2, random_state=42)


# Model Building using spaCy
nlp = spacy.blank("en")
ner = nlp.create_pipe("ner")
nlp.add_pipe(ner)


# Training the NER model
for text, entities in zip(X_train, y_train):
    doc = nlp.make_doc(text)
    example      =      spacy.training.example.Example.from_dict(doc,
{"entities": entities})
    nlp.update([example], drop=0.5)
```

```python
# Model Evaluation
y_pred = []
for text in X_test:
    doc = nlp.make_doc(text)
    y_pred.append([ent.label_ for ent in doc.ents])

# Display Model Evaluation Results
st.write("### Model Evaluation Results")
st.write(classification_report(y_test, y_pred))

# Model Deployment using Streamlit
# Assuming 'user_input' is the input text provided by the user
user_input = st.text_area("Paste your text here:")

# Predict using the trained NER model
doc = nlp.make_doc(user_input)
prediction = [ent.label_ for ent in doc.ents]

# Display Prediction
st.write("### Prediction")
st.write(f"The identified named entities in the provided text are: {', '.join(prediction)}")

# End of Code
```

This code covers named entity recognition for entities such as names of people, organizations, and locations. Users can input their text, and the model predicts the named entities. Note that this is a simplified example, and in a real-world scenario, you might need a more extensive dataset, fine-tuning, and additional considerations for

RAVINDRA KUMAR NAYAK

model selection.

PROJECT6:

Below is an end-to-end project for sentiment analysis using Natural Language Processing (NLP). This project includes parsing dummy data, preprocessing, model building using various NLP models, model evaluation, and deployment using Streamlit. The code covers sentiment analysis for positive and negative sentiments.

Python code

 # Install necessary libraries

!pip install pandas numpy scikit-learn nltk wordcloud matplotlib seaborn streamlit

 # Import libraries

import pandas as pd

import numpy as np

import nltk

from nltk.corpus import stopwords

from sklearn.model_selection import train_test_split

from sklearn.feature_extraction.text import TfidfVectorizer

from sklearn.naive_bayes import MultinomialNB

from sklearn.ensemble import RandomForestClassifier

from sklearn.svm import SVC

from sklearn.metrics import accuracy_score, classification_report

from wordcloud import WordCloud

```python
import matplotlib.pyplot as plt
import seaborn as sns
import streamlit as st

# Dummy data for sentiment analysis
# Assuming 'text' column contains review text and 'label' column
contains sentiment label
np.random.seed(42)

data = {
    'text': [' '.join(np.random.choice(words, size=50)) for _ in range(100) for words in [positive_words, negative_words]],
    'label': ['positive' for _ in range(100)] + ['negative' for _ in range(100)]
}

all_data = pd.DataFrame(data)

# Data cleaning and preprocessing
all_data['text'] = all_data['text'].apply(lambda x: ' '.join([word.lower() for word in nltk.word_tokenize(x) if word.isalpha()]))

all_data['text'] = all_data['text'].apply(lambda x: ' '.join([word for word in nltk.word_tokenize(x) if word not in stopwords.words('english')]))

# Train-test split
X_train, X_test, y_train, y_test = train_test_split(all_data['text'], all_data['label'], test_size=0.2, random_state=42)

# TF-IDF Vectorization
```

```python
tfidf_vectorizer = TfidfVectorizer(max_features=5000)
X_train_tfidf = tfidf_vectorizer.fit_transform(X_train)
X_test_tfidf = tfidf_vectorizer.transform(X_test)

# Model Building
# Naive Bayes
nb_classifier = MultinomialNB()
nb_classifier.fit(X_train_tfidf, y_train)

# Random Forest
rf_classifier = RandomForestClassifier(n_estimators=100, random_state=42)
rf_classifier.fit(X_train_tfidf, y_train)

# Support Vector Machine
svm_classifier = SVC(kernel='linear', C=1, probability=True)
svm_classifier.fit(X_train_tfidf, y_train)

# Model Evaluation
# Naive Bayes
nb_predictions = nb_classifier.predict(X_test_tfidf)
nb_accuracy = accuracy_score(y_test, nb_predictions)
nb_classification_report = classification_report(y_test, nb_predictions)

# Random Forest
rf_predictions = rf_classifier.predict(X_test_tfidf)
rf_accuracy = accuracy_score(y_test, rf_predictions)
rf_classification_report = classification_report(y_test, rf_predictions)
```

```python
# Support Vector Machine
svm_predictions = svm_classifier.predict(X_test_tfidf)
svm_accuracy = accuracy_score(y_test, svm_predictions)
svm_classification_report        =        classification_report(y_test,
svm_predictions)


# Determine the best-performing model
best_model   =   max([(nb_accuracy,   'Naive   Bayes'),   (rf_accuracy,
'Random   Forest'),   (svm_accuracy,   'Support   Vector   Machine')],
key=lambda x: x[0])


# Display Model Evaluation Results
st.write("### Model Evaluation Results")
st.write(f"Naive Bayes Accuracy: {nb_accuracy:.2f}")
st.write(f"Random Forest Accuracy: {rf_accuracy:.2f}")
st.write(f"SVM Accuracy: {svm_accuracy:.2f}")
st.write(f"Best-Performing Model: {best_model[1]}")


# Model Deployment using Streamlit
# Assuming 'user_input' is the input text provided by the user
user_input = st.text_area("Paste your review here:")


# TF-IDF Vectorization for User Input
user_input_tfidf = tfidf_vectorizer.transform([user_input])


# Predict using the best-performing model
prediction = None
if best_model[1] == 'Naive Bayes':
```

```python
    prediction = nb_classifier.predict(user_input_tfidf)
elif best_model[1] == 'Random Forest':
    prediction = rf_classifier.predict(user_input_tfidf)
elif best_model[1] == 'Support Vector Machine':
    prediction = svm_classifier.predict(user_input_tfidf)

# Display Prediction
st.write("### Prediction")
st.write(f"The predicted sentiment for the provided review is: {prediction[0]}")

# Word Cloud Visualization
# Assuming 'positive_reviews' and 'negative_reviews' are dataframes containing positive and negative reviews
positive_reviews = all_data[all_data['label'] == 'positive']
negative_reviews = all_data[all_data['label'] == 'negative']

# Positive Reviews Word Cloud
positive_text = ' '.join(positive_reviews['text'])
positive_wordcloud = WordCloud(width=800, height=400, background_color='white').generate(positive_text)
plt.figure(figsize=(10, 5))
plt.imshow(positive_wordcloud, interpolation='bilinear')
plt.title("Word Cloud for Positive Reviews")
plt.axis('off')
st.pyplot(plt)

# Negative Reviews Word Cloud
negative_text = ' '.join(negative_reviews['text'])
```

```
negative_wordcloud = WordCloud(width=800, height=400,
background_color='white').generate(negative_text)

plt.figure(figsize=(10, 5))

plt.imshow(negative_wordcloud, interpolation='bilinear')

plt.title("Word Cloud for Negative Reviews")

plt.axis('off')

st.pyplot(plt)


# Comparative Analysis and Conclusion

# Display comparative analysis results (ROC, accuracy, metrics, etc.)

# Display conclusion based on the analysis


# End of Code
```

This code covers sentiment analysis for positive and negative sentiments. Users can input their reviews, and the model predicts the sentiment. Word clouds are also displayed for positive and negative reviews. Note that this is a simplified example, and in a real-world scenario, you might need a more extensive dataset, hyperparameter tuning, and additional considerations for model selection.

PROJECT7:

Below is an end-to-end project that incorporates advanced Natural Language Processing (NLP) concepts, including text summarization and named entity recognition (NER). This project involves parsing dummy data, preprocessing, implementing advanced NLP models, and deploying the models using Streamlit.

Python code

 # Install necessary libraries

!pip install pandas numpy scikit-learn nltk spacy streamlit transformers

 # Import libraries

import pandas as pd

import numpy as np

import nltk

import spacy

from sklearn.model_selection import train_test_split

from sklearn.metrics import classification_report

from transformers import pipeline

import streamlit as st

 # Dummy data for advanced NLP project

 # Assuming 'text' column contains articles and 'entities' column contains named entities

```python
np.random.seed(42)

data = {
    'text': [' '.join(np.random.choice(words, size=100)) for _ in range(100) for words in [people_names, company_names, locations]],
    'entities': [['PERSON'] for _ in range(100)] + [['ORG'] for _ in range(100)] + [['GPE'] for _ in range(100)]
}


all_data = pd.DataFrame(data)

# Data preprocessing for NER
all_data['text'] = all_data['text'].apply(lambda x: ' '.join([word.lower() for word in nltk.word_tokenize(x) if word.isalpha()]))


# Train-test split for NER
X_train_ner, X_test_ner, y_train_ner, y_test_ner = train_test_split(all_data['text'], all_data['entities'], test_size=0.2, random_state=42)


# Model Building for NER using spaCy
nlp_ner = spacy.blank("en")
ner_nlp = nlp_ner.create_pipe("ner")
nlp_ner.add_pipe(ner_nlp)

# Training the NER model
for text, entities in zip(X_train_ner, y_train_ner):
    doc = nlp_ner.make_doc(text)
    example = spacy.training.example.Example.from_dict(doc,
```

```python
    {"entities": entities})
    nlp_ner.update([example], drop=0.5)

# Model Evaluation for NER
y_pred_ner = []
for text in X_test_ner:
    doc = nlp_ner.make_doc(text)
    y_pred_ner.append([ent.label_ for ent in doc.ents])

# Display NER Model Evaluation Results
st.write("### Named Entity Recognition (NER) Model Evaluation Results")
st.write(classification_report(y_test_ner, y_pred_ner))

# Model Deployment for NER using Streamlit
# Assuming 'user_input_ner' is the input text provided by the user
user_input_ner = st.text_area("Paste your text here for Named Entity Recognition:")

# Predict using the trained NER model
doc_ner = nlp_ner.make_doc(user_input_ner)
prediction_ner = [ent.label_ for ent in doc_ner.ents]

# Display NER Prediction
st.write("### NER Prediction")
st.write(f"The identified named entities in the provided text are: {', '.join(prediction_ner)}")

# Text Summarization using Transformers
```

```python
summarizer = pipeline("summarization")

# Assuming 'user_input_summarization' is the input text provided by the user
user_input_summarization = st.text_area("Paste your text here for Text Summarization:")

# Summarize the user input
summary = summarizer(user_input_summarization, max_length=100, min_length=50, length_penalty=2.0, num_beams=4, early_stopping=True)
generated_summary = summary[0]['summary_text']

# Display Summarization Results
st.write("### Text Summarization Results")
st.write(f"The summarized version of the provided text is: \n{generated_summary}")

# End of Code
```

This code integrates named entity recognition (NER) using spaCy and text summarization using the Transformers library. Users can input text for NER and text summarization, and the models provide the respective outputs. Note that this is a simplified example, and in a real-world scenario, you might need more extensive datasets and fine-tuning for these advanced NLP tasks.

PROJECT8:

Below is an end-to-end project that focuses on sentiment analysis and emotion detection using advanced Natural Language Processing (NLP) techniques. This project includes parsing dummy data, preprocessing, implementing advanced NLP models, and deploying the models using Streamlit.

Python code

```python
# Install necessary libraries
!pip install pandas numpy scikit-learn nltk transformers streamlit

# Import libraries
import pandas as pd
import numpy as np
import nltk
from sklearn.model_selection import train_test_split
from sklearn.metrics import classification_report
from transformers import pipeline
import streamlit as st

# Dummy data for sentiment analysis and emotion detection
# Assuming 'text' column contains sentences and 'sentiment'/'emotion' column contains corresponding labels
np.random.seed(42)
```

```python
data = {
    'text': [' '.join(np.random.choice(words, size=15)) for _ in range(100) for words in [positive_words, negative_words]],
    'sentiment': ['positive' for _ in range(100)] + ['negative' for _ in range(100)],
    'emotion': ['happy' for _ in range(50)] + ['sad' for _ in range(50)]
}

all_data = pd.DataFrame(data)

# Data preprocessing for sentiment analysis
all_data['text'] = all_data['text'].apply(lambda x: ' '.join([word.lower() for word in nltk.word_tokenize(x) if word.isalpha()]))

# Train-test split for sentiment analysis
X_train_sentiment, X_test_sentiment, y_train_sentiment, y_test_sentiment = train_test_split(all_data['text'], all_data['sentiment'], test_size=0.2, random_state=42)

# Model Building for Sentiment Analysis using Transformers
sentiment_classifier = pipeline("sentiment-analysis")

# Model Evaluation for Sentiment Analysis
y_pred_sentiment = [result['label'] for result in sentiment_classifier(X_test_sentiment)]

# Display Sentiment Analysis Model Evaluation Results
st.write("### Sentiment Analysis Model Evaluation Results")
st.write(classification_report(y_test_sentiment, y_pred_sentiment))
```

```python
# Model Deployment for Sentiment Analysis using Streamlit
# Assuming 'user_input_sentiment' is the input text provided by the user
user_input_sentiment = st.text_area("Paste your text here for Sentiment Analysis:")

# Predict using the Sentiment Analysis model
prediction_sentiment = sentiment_classifier(user_input_sentiment)[0]['label']

# Display Sentiment Analysis Prediction
st.write("### Sentiment Analysis Prediction")
st.write(f"The predicted sentiment for the provided text is: {prediction_sentiment}")

# Train-test split for emotion detection
X_train_emotion, X_test_emotion, y_train_emotion, y_test_emotion = train_test_split(all_data['text'], all_data['emotion'], test_size=0.2, random_state=42)

# Model Building for Emotion Detection using Transformers
emotion_classifier = pipeline("text-classification", model="nlptown/bert-base-multilingual-uncased-emotion")

# Model Evaluation for Emotion Detection
y_pred_emotion = [result['label'] for result in emotion_classifier(X_test_emotion)]

# Display Emotion Detection Model Evaluation Results
st.write("### Emotion Detection Model Evaluation Results")
```

```python
st.write(classification_report(y_test_emotion, y_pred_emotion))

# Model Deployment for Emotion Detection using Streamlit
# Assuming 'user_input_emotion' is the input text provided by the user
user_input_emotion = st.text_area("Paste your text here for Emotion
Detection:")


# Predict using the Emotion Detection model
prediction_emotion   =   emotion_classifier(user_input_emotion)[0]
['label']


# Display Emotion Detection Prediction
st.write("### Emotion Detection Prediction")
st.write(f"The   predicted   emotion   for   the   provided   text   is:
{prediction_emotion}")


# End of Code
```

This code integrates sentiment analysis and emotion detection using the Transformers library. Users can input text for both sentiment analysis and emotion detection, and the models provide the respective outputs. Note that this is a simplified example, and in a real-world scenario, you might need more extensive datasets and fine-tuning for these advanced NLP tasks.

PROJECT9:

Below is an end-to-end project that focuses on text classification using a BERT-based model for a custom task, such as topic classification. This project includes parsing dummy data, preprocessing, implementing advanced NLP models, and deploying the models using Streamlit.

Python code

 # Install necessary libraries

!pip install pandas numpy scikit-learn transformers streamlit

 # Import libraries

import pandas as pd

import numpy as np

from sklearn.model_selection import train_test_split

from sklearn.metrics import classification_report

from transformers import BertTokenizer, BertForSequenceClassification, AdamW

from torch.utils.data import DataLoader, TensorDataset

import torch

from tqdm import tqdm

import streamlit as st

 # Dummy data for text classification

 # Assuming 'text' column contains articles and 'category' column

```python
contains corresponding labels
np.random.seed(42)

data = {
    'text': [' '.join(np.random.choice(words, size=100)) for _
in range(100) for words in [technology_words, sports_words,
politics_words]],
    'category': ['technology' for _ in range(50)] + ['sports' for _ in
range(25)] + ['politics' for _ in range(25)]
}

all_data = pd.DataFrame(data)

# Data preprocessing for text classification
all_data['text']       =       all_data['text'].apply(lambda       x:       '
'.join([word.lower() for word in x.split()]))

# Train-test split for text classification
X_train_text,    X_test_text,    y_train_text,    y_test_text    =
train_test_split(all_data['text'],    all_data['category'],    test_size=0.2,
random_state=42)

# Tokenization and DataLoader
tokenizer    =    BertTokenizer.from_pretrained('bert-base-uncased',
truncation=True, padding=True)

X_train_encoded                =                tokenizer(X_train_text.tolist(),
return_tensors='pt',    max_length=128,    padding='max_length',
truncation=True)

X_test_encoded = tokenizer(X_test_text.tolist(), return_tensors='pt',
max_length=128, padding='max_length', truncation=True)
```

```python
y_train_encoded = torch.tensor([{'technology': 0, 'sports': 1, 'politics': 2}[label] for label in y_train_text])
y_test_encoded = torch.tensor([{'technology': 0, 'sports': 1, 'politics': 2}[label] for label in y_test_text])

train_dataset = TensorDataset(X_train_encoded['input_ids'], X_train_encoded['attention_mask'], y_train_encoded)
test_dataset = TensorDataset(X_test_encoded['input_ids'], X_test_encoded['attention_mask'], y_test_encoded)

train_dataloader = DataLoader(train_dataset, batch_size=8, shuffle=True)
test_dataloader = DataLoader(test_dataset, batch_size=8, shuffle=False)

# Model Building for Text Classification using BERT
model = BertForSequenceClassification.from_pretrained('bert-base-uncased', num_labels=3)
optimizer = AdamW(model.parameters(), lr=2e-5)

device = torch.device('cuda' if torch.cuda.is_available() else 'cpu')
model.to(device)

# Training the model
num_epochs = 3
for epoch in range(num_epochs):
    model.train()
    for batch in tqdm(train_dataloader, desc=f'Epoch {epoch + 1}/{num_epochs}'):
        input_ids, attention_mask, labels = batch
```

```python
        input_ids, attention_mask, labels = input_ids.to(device),
attention_mask.to(device), labels.to(device)

        optimizer.zero_grad()
        outputs = model(input_ids, attention_mask=attention_mask,
labels=labels)
        loss = outputs.loss
        loss.backward()
        optimizer.step()

# Model Evaluation for Text Classification
model.eval()
predictions = []
true_labels = []

with torch.no_grad():
    for batch in tqdm(test_dataloader, desc='Evaluating'):
        input_ids, attention_mask, labels = batch
        input_ids, attention_mask, labels = input_ids.to(device),
attention_mask.to(device), labels.to(device)

        outputs = model(input_ids, attention_mask=attention_mask)
        logits = outputs.logits
        predictions.extend(torch.argmax(logits,
axis=1).cpu().numpy())
        true_labels.extend(labels.cpu().numpy())

# Display Text Classification Model Evaluation Results
st.write("### Text Classification Model Evaluation Results")
```

```python
st.write(classification_report(true_labels, predictions, target_names=['technology', 'sports', 'politics']))

# Model Deployment for Text Classification using Streamlit
# Assuming 'user_input_text' is the input text provided by the user
user_input_text = st.text_area("Paste your text here for Text Classification:")

# Tokenize and Encode User Input
user_input_encoded = tokenizer(user_input_text, return_tensors='pt', max_length=128, padding='max_length', truncation=True)
user_input_encoded = {key: value.to(device) for key, value in user_input_encoded.items()}

# Predict using the Text Classification model
model.eval()
with torch.no_grad():
    output = model(**user_input_encoded)
    prediction_text = torch.argmax(output.logits, axis=1).item()

# Map prediction index back to category label
category_mapping = {0: 'technology', 1: 'sports', 2: 'politics'}
predicted_category = category_mapping[prediction_text]

# Display Text Classification Prediction
st.write("### Text Classification Prediction")
st.write(f"The predicted category for the provided text is: {predicted_category}")

# End of Code
```

This code uses a BERT-based model for text classification with categories such as technology, sports, and politics. Users can input text, and the model predicts the category. Note that this is a simplified example, and in a real-world scenario, you might need more extensive datasets and fine-tuning for your specific text classification task.

PROJECT10:

Below is an end-to-end project that focuses on document clustering using unsupervised learning techniques like K-means clustering. This project includes parsing dummy data, preprocessing, implementing unsupervised learning models, and deploying the models using Streamlit.

Python code

 # Install necessary libraries

!pip install pandas numpy scikit-learn streamlit

 # Import libraries

import pandas as pd

import numpy as np

from sklearn.feature_extraction.text import TfidfVectorizer

from sklearn.cluster import KMeans

from sklearn.decomposition import PCA

import streamlit as st

 # Dummy data for document clustering

np.random.seed(42)

data = {

*   'text': [' '.join(np.random.choice(words, size=50)) for _ in range(100) for words in [tech_words, sports_words, politics_words]],*

```python
    'category': ['technology' for _ in range(50)] + ['sports' for _ in range(25)] + ['politics' for _ in range(25)]
}

all_data = pd.DataFrame(data)

# Data preprocessing for document clustering
all_data['text'] = all_data['text'].apply(lambda x: ' '.join([word.lower() for word in x.split()]))

# Feature extraction using TF-IDF
vectorizer = TfidfVectorizer(stop_words='english', max_features=1000)
X = vectorizer.fit_transform(all_data['text'])

# Dimensionality reduction using PCA
pca = PCA(n_components=2)
X_pca = pca.fit_transform(X.toarray())

# Model Building for Document Clustering using K-means
kmeans = KMeans(n_clusters=3, random_state=42)
all_data['cluster'] = kmeans.fit_predict(X)

# Model Deployment for Document Clustering using Streamlit
# Assuming 'user_input_cluster' is the input text provided by the user
user_input_cluster = st.text_area("Paste your text here for Document Clustering:")

# Feature extraction for user input
user_input_vectorized = vectorizer.transform([user_input_cluster])
```

```
# Dimensionality reduction for user input
user_input_pca = pca.transform(user_input_vectorized.toarray())

# Predict using the Document Clustering model
user_input_prediction = kmeans.predict(user_input_vectorized)

# Display Document Clustering Prediction
st.write("### Document Clustering Prediction")
st.write(f"The predicted cluster for the provided text is: {user_input_prediction[0]}")

# Display Document Clustering Visualization
st.write("### Document Clustering Visualization")
st.scatter_chart(pd.DataFrame(X_pca, columns=['PC1', 'PC2']))

# End of Code
```

This code uses unsupervised learning techniques for document clustering. Users can input text, and the model predicts the cluster to which the input text belongs. The visualization section displays the document clustering results in a 2D scatter chart. Note that this is a simplified example, and in a real-world scenario, you might need more extensive datasets and fine-tuning for your specific document clustering task.

let's break down the basic structure of the fundamentals of each code and explain key terms related to Natural Language Processing (NLP) with examples.

Project 1: Python Fundamentals

Basic Structure:

Introduction (Chapter 1): Overview of Python's origins and philosophy.

Setting Up (Chapter 2): Guide for installing Python and exploring the interpreter.

"Hello, World!" (Chapter 3): Introduction to Python syntax and structure.

Variables and Data Types (Chapter 4): Explanation of variables and data types.

Control Flow (Chapter 5): Introduction to if statements and loops.

Functions (Chapter 6): Understanding functions and modular programming.

Pythonic Ways (Chapter 7): Exploring Python's elegant coding style.

Handling Errors (Chapter 8): Introduction to exception handling.

Python Libraries (Chapter 9): Overview of popular libraries like NumPy and Pandas.

Object-Oriented Programming (Chapter 10): Introduction to OOP concepts.

Key Terms:

Pythonic: Writing code in a way that follows Python's conventions and idioms.

Example: Using list comprehensions instead of traditional for-loops for concise code.

Exception Handling: Managing errors in a program to prevent crashes.

Example: Using try-except blocks to catch and handle potential errors.

NumPy: Library for numerical operations in Python, essential for scientific computing.

Example: Creating arrays and performing mathematical operations with NumPy.

Pandas: Library for data manipulation and analysis.

Example: Reading a CSV file into a Pandas DataFrame and analyzing data.

Object-Oriented Programming (OOP): A programming paradigm using objects with properties and methods.

Example: Creating classes like 'Car' with attributes (color, model) and methods (start, stop).

Project 2: NLP Fundamentals

Basic Structure:

NLP Origins (Chapter 1): Introduction to Natural Language Processing.

Text Preprocessing (Chapter 2): Techniques for preparing textual data.

Exploratory Data Analysis (Chapter 3): Analyzing word frequencies, n-grams, sentiment distributions.

Model Building (Chapter 4): Implementing NLP models.

Model Evaluation (Chapter 5): Understanding metrics for model performance.

Model Deployment (Chapter 6): Taking models from notebooks to real-world applications.

Comparative Analysis (Chapter 7): Comparing different NLP models.

Holistic Mastery (Chapter 8): Summarizing NLP concepts.

Key Terms:

Tokenization: Breaking down text into smaller units (tokens).

Example: Tokenizing the sentence "Hello, World!" results in ["Hello", ",", "World", "!"].

TF-IDF (Term Frequency-Inverse Document Frequency): A numerical statistic to represent the importance of a word in a document.

Example: In a document about Python, "Python" will have a high TF-IDF score.

Named Entity Recognition (NER): Identifying and classifying named entities in text.

Example: In "Apple Inc. is headquartered in Cupertino," NER identifies "Apple Inc." as an organization.

Word Embeddings: Representing words as vectors in a continuous vector space.

Example: Word embeddings can capture semantic relationships, like the vector for "king" being similar to "queen."

Sentiment Analysis: Determining the sentiment (positive, negative, neutral) expressed in a piece of text.

Example: "I love this product!" expresses positive sentiment.

Text Summarization: Condensing a piece of text while retaining its main points.

Example: Summarizing a news article to capture its essential information.

Streamlit: A Python library for creating web applications for data science and machine learning.

Example: Deploying an NLP model in a Streamlit app for user interaction.

Project 3: Advanced NLP (Sentiment Analysis and Emotion Detection)

Basic Structure:

Sentiment Analysis (Chapter 1): Analyzing sentiment in text.

Emotion Detection (Chapter 2): Identifying emotions in text.

Key Terms:

Pipeline: A sequence of data processing steps.

Example: In Transformers, a sentiment analysis pipeline processes input text to predict sentiment.

Bert-Based Model: A type of deep learning model based on the Transformer architecture, known for its effectiveness in NLP tasks.

Example: The sentiment analysis model in Transformers is Bert-based.

Tokenization (Advanced): In-depth breakdown of text into tokens.

Example: Tokenizing not only words but also subwords for a finer level of analysis.

ROC (Receiver Operating Characteristic) Curve: A graphical representation of a model's ability to discriminate between positive and negative classes.

Example: Evaluating the performance of a sentiment analysis model using an ROC curve.

Named Entity Recognition (Advanced): Fine-tuning NER models for specific tasks.

Example: Adapting a general NER model to recognize domain-specific entities.

Project 4: Document Clustering

Basic Structure:

Document Clustering (Chapter 1): Introduction to unsupervised learning for clustering documents.

Key Terms:

TF-IDF (Advanced): Feature extraction technique for text data.

Example: Calculating TF-IDF scores for words in a collection of documents.

K-Means Clustering: An unsupervised learning algorithm for partitioning data into clusters.

Example: Grouping documents into clusters based on their content.

PCA (Principal Component Analysis): Dimensionality reduction technique.

Example: Reducing the dimensionality of TF-IDF vectors for visualization.

Cluster Visualization: Representing clusters visually.

Example: Plotting documents in a 2D space based on their PCA-transformed features.

User Input for Clustering (Chapter 2): Allowing users to input text for clustering.

Example: Users entering a piece of text to determine its cluster.

Project 5-9: Additional Projects (Resume Classification, Role-based Classification, etc.)

These projects follow a similar structure, introducing a specific NLP task and showcasing its implementation.

Project 10: Advanced NLP Concepts

Basic Structure:

Advanced NLP Concepts (Chapter 1): Exploring advanced NLP techniques.

Key Terms:

Transfer Learning in NLP: Using pre-trained models for specific NLP tasks.

Example: Fine-tuning a BERT model for a sentiment analysis task.

Named Entity Recognition (Advanced): Customizing NER models for specialized entities.

Example: Adapting an NER model to recognize medical entities.

Document Embeddings: Representing entire documents as vectors.

Example: Creating embeddings for entire articles instead of individual words.

This structure provides a comprehensive overview of each project's focus, and the key terms offer an understanding of important concepts in NLP.

BELOW IS A GLOSSARY OF TERMS RELATED TO PYTHON PROGRAMMING AND NATURAL LANGUAGE PROCESSING (NLP):

Python Programming Glossary:

Python: A high-level, versatile programming language.

Interpreter: A program that executes Python code line by line.

Hello, World!: A simple introductory program printing "Hello, World!" to the console.

Variables: Containers for storing data.

Data Types: Categories of data, e.g., int, float, str.

Control Flow: The order in which statements are executed in a program.

Functions: Blocks of reusable code.

Pythonic: Writing code following Python conventions and idioms.

Exception Handling: Managing errors during program execution.

NumPy: Library for numerical operations.

Pandas: Library for data manipulation and analysis.

Object-Oriented Programming (OOP): A programming paradigm using objects with properties and methods.

Natural Language Processing (NLP) Glossary:

NLP (Natural Language Processing): A field of AI focusing on interactions between computers and humans using natural language.

Tokenization: Breaking text into smaller units (tokens).

TF-IDF (Term Frequency-Inverse Document Frequency): A numerical statistic representing word importance in a document.

Named Entity Recognition (NER): Identifying and classifying named entities in text.

Word Embeddings: Representing words as vectors in a continuous vector space.

Sentiment Analysis: Determining the sentiment (positive, negative, neutral) expressed in text.

Text Summarization: Condensing text while retaining main points.

Streamlit: A Python library for creating web applications for data science and machine learning.

BERT (Bidirectional Encoder Representations from Transformers): A pre-trained transformer-based NLP model.

Pipeline: A sequence of data processing steps.

ROC Curve (Receiver Operating Characteristic): A graphical representation of a model's ability to discriminate between classes.

Transfer Learning in NLP: Using pre-trained models for specific NLP tasks.

PCA (Principal Component Analysis): A dimensionality reduction technique.

K-Means Clustering: An unsupervised learning algorithm for partitioning data into clusters.

Document Embeddings: Representing entire documents as vectors.

Advanced NLP Glossary:

Text Classification: Assigning predefined categories to text.

Embedding Layer: A layer in neural networks that learns word representations.

LSTM (Long Short-Term Memory): A type of recurrent neural network.

Attention Mechanism: Focusing on specific parts of input data in neural networks.

Hyperparameter Tuning: Adjusting parameters to optimize model performance.

Fine-Tuning: Adjusting pre-trained models for specific tasks.

Grid Search: A method to search hyperparameter combinations for the best model performance.

Zero-Shot Learning: Training models to perform tasks without explicit examples.

Named Entity Recognition (Advanced): Fine-tuning NER models for specific tasks.

Document Clustering Glossary:

Clustering: Grouping data points based on similarity.

TF-IDF (Advanced): A feature extraction technique for text data.

PCA (Advanced): A dimensionality reduction technique.

Cluster Visualization: Representing clusters visually.

User Input for Clustering: Allowing users to input text for clustering.

Role-Based Classification Glossary:

Role-Based Classification: Assigning roles based on text content.

Dummy Dataset: A simulated dataset for testing and demonstration purposes.

Model Evaluation: Assessing the performance of machine learning models.

Advanced NLP Concepts Glossary:

Transfer Learning in NLP: Using pre-trained models for specific NLP tasks.

Document Embeddings: Representing entire documents as vectors.

Project-Specific Glossary:

Resume Classification: Assigning categories to resumes based on content.

Role-Based Classification: Assigning roles to text based on content.

Miscellaneous Glossary:

ROC Curve: A graphical representation of a model's ability to discriminate between classes.

Advanced NER: Customizing NER models for specialized entities.

Project: A task with a specific goal and planned outcomes.

Collaboratory (Colab): A cloud-based platform for developing and running Python code.

TensorFlow: An open-source machine learning framework.

Additional NLP Terms:

Parsing: Analyzing text syntactically.

Preprocessing: Cleaning and organizing data before analysis.

EDA (Exploratory Data Analysis): Analyzing data for insights.

Algorithm: A step-by-step procedure for solving problems.

Model Building: Constructing machine learning models.

Model Deployment: Implementing models for real-world use.

EDA (Exploratory Data Analysis): Analyzing data for insights.

Clustering: Grouping data points based on similarity.

TF-IDF (Term Frequency-Inverse Document Frequency): A numerical statistic representing word importance in a document.

K-Means Clustering: An unsupervised learning algorithm for partitioning data into clusters.

PCA (Principal Component Analysis): A dimensionality reduction technique.

User Input: Information provided by users for analysis.

Visualization: Representing data graphically for better understanding.

Feature Extraction: Transforming raw data into a format suitable for modeling.

Unsupervised Learning: Learning patterns in data without labeled outcomes.

Supervised Learning: Training models with labeled data to make predictions.

Fine-Tuning: Adjusting pre-trained models for specific tasks.

Grid Search: A method to search hyperparameter combinations for the best model performance.

Zero-Shot Learning: Training models to perform tasks without explicit examples.

LSTM (Long Short-Term Memory): A type of recurrent neural network.

Attention Mechanism: Focusing on specific parts of input data in neural networks.

Hyperparameter Tuning: Adjusting parameters to optimize model performance.

Collaboratory and Streamlit Terms:

Collaboratory (Colab): A cloud-based platform for developing and running Python code.

Streamlit: A Python library for creating web applications for data science and machine learning.

Advanced NLP Concepts:

Transfer Learning in NLP: Using pre-trained models for specific NLP tasks.

Document Embeddings: Representing entire documents as vectors.

Project-Specific Terms:

Resume Classification: Assigning categories to resumes based on content.

Role-Based Classification: Assigning roles to text based on content.

Miscellaneous Terms:

ROC Curve: A graphical representation of a model's ability to discriminate between classes.

Advanced NER: Customizing NER models for specialized entities.

Project: A task with a specific goal and planned outcomes.

TensorFlow: An open-source machine learning framework.

Word Embeddings: Representing words as vectors in a continuous vector space.

Named Entity Recognition (NER): Identifying and classifying named entities in text.

Sentiment Analysis: Determining the sentiment (positive, negative, neutral) expressed in a piece of text.

Text Summarization: Condensing a piece of text while retaining its main points.

Bert-Based Model: A type of deep learning model based on the Transformer architecture, known for its effectiveness in NLP tasks.

Tokenization (Advanced): In-depth breakdown of text into tokens.

ROC (Receiver Operating Characteristic) Curve: A graphical representation of a model's ability to discriminate between positive and negative classes.

Named Entity Recognition (Advanced): Fine-tuning NER models for specific tasks.

Pipeline: A sequence of data processing steps.

Grid Search: A method to search hyperparameter combinations for the best model performance.

Zero-Shot Learning: Training models to perform tasks without explicit examples.

BERT (Bidirectional Encoder Representations from Transformers): A pre-trained transformer-based NLP model.

Clustering: Grouping data points based on similarity.

TF-IDF (Advanced): A feature extraction technique for text data.

K-Means Clustering: An unsupervised learning algorithm for partitioning data into clusters.

PCA (Advanced): A dimensionality reduction technique.

This glossary covers a wide range of terms related to both Python programming and Natural Language Processing (NLP), providing a comprehensive understanding of key concepts.

ACKNOWLEDGMENT

Writing a book is a journey that involves the support and encouragement of numerous individuals who contribute to its realization. As I reflect on the completion of this book on Natural Language Processing (NLP), I want to express my gratitude to those who have been instrumental in its creation.

First and foremost, I extend my sincere appreciation to the community of researchers, educators, and practitioners in the field of NLP. Your continuous efforts in advancing the boundaries of language understanding and processing have been a constant source of inspiration.

I am grateful for the mentorship and guidance whose expertise has been invaluable in shaping the content of this book. Your insights and constructive feedback have significantly enriched the quality of the material.

I would like to extend my thanks to , whose dedication and professionalism have played a crucial role in bringing this book to fruition. Your commitment to excellence and attention to detail have been evident throughout the publishing process.

To my family and friends, thank you for your unwavering support and understanding during the long hours spent researching, writing, and editing. Your encouragement has been the driving force behind this endeavor.

Last but not least, I express my gratitude to the readers of this book. It is my sincere hope that the knowledge shared within these pages serves as a valuable resource for your exploration of the fascinating world of Natural Language Processing.

Thank you all for being a part of this journey.

SUMMARY

"Unveiling NLP" is a comprehensive guide that navigates readers through the intricate landscape of Natural Language Processing (NLP). Covering fundamental concepts like tokenization and sentiment analysis, the book progresses to advanced topics, including model building, evaluation, and deployment. With hands-on projects, it demystifies NLP, making it accessible to both technical and non-technical readers. The journey concludes with a comparative analysis, empowering readers to choose the most effective models. Whether delving into text clustering or role-based classification, this book transforms NLP from a complex subject into a piece of cake, fostering a deeper understanding and appreciation for language processing intricacies.